Law at Work

- facts no trade unionist, personnel officer, employer or employee should ignore
- concise easy-to-read style
- assumes no previous knowledge of law
- emphasis on everyday situations in the workplace

Safety Representatives

Safety representatives have lately assumed much greater importance in the workplace. This book examines in detail their appointment, their functions, their attendance at safety committees and the significance of the inspections they are empowered to carry out. Finally, it points to possible future development of their role in promoting the welfare of an organisation's work-force.

AUSTRALIA
The Law Book Company Ltd.
Sydney : Melbourne : Brisbane

CANADA AND U.S.A.
The Carswell Company Ltd.
Agincourt, Ontario

INDIA
N.M. Tripathi Private Ltd.
Bombay
and
Eastern Law House Private Ltd.
Calcutta
M.P.P. House
Bangalore

ISRAEL
Steimatzky's Agency Ltd.
Jerusalem : Tel Aviv : Haifa

MALAYSIA : SINGAPORE : BRUNEI
Malayan Law Journal (Pte.) Ltd.
Singapore

NEW ZEALAND
Sweet and Maxwell (N.Z.) Ltd.
Auckland

PAKISTAN
Pakistan Law House
Karachi

Contents

Abbreviations and Terminology

ACAS	The Advisory, Conciliation and Arbitration Service
CAC	The Central Arbitration Committee
The Code	The Health and Safety Commission's Code of Practice on Safety Representatives
EMAS	The Employment Medical Advisory Service
EPA	The Employment Protection Act 1975
EPCA	The Employment Protection (Consolidation) Act 1978
The Guidance Notes or GN	The Health and Safety Commission's Guidance Notes on Safety Representatives
HASAWA	The Health and Safety at Work Act 1974
HSC	The Health and Safety Commission
HSE	The Health and Safety Executive
The Regulations or Regs.	The Safety Representatives and Safety Committees Regulations 1977
s. or ss.	section or sections of a statute (*e.g.* HASAWA, s. 2)
The SC Guidance Notes or SCGN	The Health and Safety Commission's Guidance Notes on Safety Committees
TULRA	Trade Union and Labour Relations Act 1974
Constituency	The bargaining unit to which safety representatives and shop stewards are answerable.
Employers	This includes limited companies, statutory bodies, local authorities, etc., as well as individual employers.

Establishment	A separate physical unit in an undertaking (*e.g.* a shop, office block or factory).
He	This is not intended to suggest that any position is not equally open to women.
Management	Includes supervisors or those to whom an employer devolves authority. Sometimes used here as synonymous with "employer."
Shop stewards	Used here to refer to all part-time union officials other than safety representatives.
Undertaking	All the departments, branches or plants of an employer.

General Editor of the Series: Paul O'Higgins, M.A.Ph.D.
Advisory Editor: John Broadbent, M.A.

Other Titles in the Series

Employment Contracts
Going to Law
Trade Unions
Union Members
Wages and Salaries

1 Introduction

What is a safety representative?

Safety representatives are relatively new and unfamiliar figures in most workplaces. Like shop stewards they are appointed to represent their workmates' or constituents' interests; and as part-time union officials both stewards and representatives have similar relationships to their unions. Unlike shop stewards, however, the range of a safety representative's responsibilities is limited to health, safety and welfare at work, but within these limits his functions are fairly similar to a shop steward's: he investigates his workmates' complaints and makes representations to management on their behalf; he inspects the workplace; and he receives information from the employer or factory inspector to pass on to his members; however, unlike shop stewards safety representatives have the backing of quite detailed powers provided by law.

A safety representative is responsible to his union, not to management. By contrast other people with a specialist interest in safety, such as safety officers, are responsible to the employer. Obviously by helping to achieve a safe and healthy workplace, safety representatives assist their employer to discharge his primary duty to provide a safe, healthy working environment. On some occasions, though, there may be conflict between, say, a safety representative's view that a piece of machinery is a source of danger and needs to be replaced, and the employer's view that it is perfectly safe. Despite their extensive legal rights, safety representatives generally seek to settle such disputes internally by collective bargaining because few of their legal powers are enforceable through the courts. This reliance on collective bargaining is another feature that safety representatives share in common with shop stewards. However, if collective bargaining proves ineffective, safety representatives additionally have the persuasive and enforcement powers of the inspectorates to fall back on.

Safety committees

This book also deals with safety representatives' relationships with safety committees (see Chap. 6). Safety committees have long existed in many undertakings to provide a machinery for consultation between workers and management on aspects of health, safety and welfare at work. Until October 1978 such committees were established voluntarily, but now their establishment can also be requested by two safety representatives. In either case, a safety committee will monitor the general state of health and safety at work in that particular establishment, while the safety representatives (if any) concern themselves with the more specific tasks described above.

The regulation of health and safety at work prior to 1974

Since the 1830s, Acts of Parliament or "statutes" have laid on employers detailed duties, for example to fence machinery, ensure adequate ventilation, heating and lighting, provide safe lifting tackle, and keep floors, stairs and passages free from obstruction. Breach of these statutory duties renders the employer liable to prosecution by official inspectors in the criminal courts, and on conviction, punishment takes the form of fines. Alternatively an injured employee can often sue in a *civil* action for monetary compensation ("damages") which is recoverable from the employer who is at fault.

Civil actions for damages take two forms:

(a) an action for breach of an employer's statutory duties (*e.g.* his duty under the Factories Act to guard dangerous machines) as a result of which an employee is injured. Such actions are called "actions for breach of statutory duty," but prior to 1974 they were only available to those working in certain premises, such as factories, mines and quarries or (much later) shops and offices, which were covered by a statute laying on the employer specific duties.

(b) an action "at common law" for negligence, that is an action against an employer for failure to comply with standards laid down by judges in previous cases, as a result of which a worker suffers injury. These judge-made standards impose broad duties which cover some of the same ground covered in more detail by statutes like the Factories Act. So, for example, judges have laid down that employers must take reasonable care to provide safe systems of work, competent staff and safe plant and machinery.

Defects in the pre-1974 system and the Robens Report

The continuing high figures of occupational injuries and illness made it clear that the emphasis on punishment and compensation after the event did little to reduce the terrible toll of illness and accidents. The legislation was excessively complex and detailed, yet it permitted uncertainty and different standards in different industries, and created confusing dividing lines between the responsibilities of the different inspectorates. In any case, there were so few inspectors that they were only able to visit factories on average once in four years, and when they did find defects, they preferred to rely on persuasion and cajolery rather than enforcement by prosecution. The effect of prosecutions was further reduced by the low level of fines. Lastly, more than eight million workers were not covered by any kind of safety legislation at all.

The Committee, headed by Lord Robens, appointed to look into these matters in 1970, recommended greater involvement of workpeople themselves. A natural identity or interest in health and safety was found to exist between the two sides of industry, which provided much scope for constructive discussion, joint inspection, and participation in working out solutions, to which a safety representative's knowledge of habits and attitudes on the shopfloor could contribute especially valuable expertise (para. 66). This led the Committee to recommend (at paras. 68-74) the enactment of:

(a) a statutory duty on employers to consult with employees or their representatives on measures for promoting safety and health at work and to provide arrangements for the participation of employees in the further development of such measures. This, of course, was the concept of the safety representative; and

(b) a legal obligation on employers to set out their safety and health policies and rules in writing and to make such policies available to all employees as a means of putting pressure on employers to raise their standards. This recommendation saw the light of day in the statutory requirement of an employer's safety policy described in more detail on page 45.

The Health and Safety at Work Act 1974 ("HASAWA")

Many of the recommendations of the Robens Report were incorporated in HASAWA. A basic change was its regulation of the conditions of people "at work" rather than of those working in certain types of premises. So within the Act's protection are eight million so-called "new entrants" not previously covered because, say, they do not work in factories or offices or shops or railway premises, but in schools, hospitals, various forms of transport, agriculture, off-shore installations and in many non-office local government jobs, such as librarianship and refuse collection. This avoids many of the difficult distinctions that had to be drawn under the pre-1974 legislation. HASAWA also covers the self-employed, and it extends, too, to Northern Ireland.

In place of the detailed duties of the Factories Act, HASAWA lays down duties expressed in general terms similar to the standards established by judges at common law. These no longer apply merely to employers in relation to their employees, but also to persons whose health and safety may be affected by the employer's undertaking (*e.g.* visitors) (s. 3), or by its harmful emissions into the atmosphere (s. 5), or to sub-contractors and others lawfully on the employer's premises. Wide duties are laid on designers, manufacturers, importers, and suppliers of articles (s. 6), and an employee is also bound "to take reasonable care for the health and safety of himself and of other persons who may be affected by his acts or omissions at work" (s. 7).

These broadly expressed duties on employers and others are, however, not absolute, but apply (with the exception of ss. 5 and 7) only so far as is "reasonably practicable." In assessing what is reasonably practicable compliance with his statutory duties, an employer must persuade a court that the time, trouble and expense in complying with the standard outweigh the consequences that might flow from non-compliance. For instance, it may constitute reasonably practicable compliance with his duty to keep a factory floor safe if an employer covers it with sawdust after a sudden storm has caused flooding. Although this would still leave the floor relatively unsafe, the only alternative might be to close the factory entirely with all that this might involve in lost wages and production.

A breach of such general duties can only result in criminal prosecutions brought by the inspectorate (see below); it cannot be the grounds for an action for breach of statutory duty by an injured individual. However, such an action may be brought under health and safety regulations made under HASAWA (see below).

Regulations, codes of practice and guidance notes

The emphasis on a broad framework of general duties in HASAWA means that other legislation has to supply the sort of detail that is required to regulate health and safety at work in the widely varying circumstances of different workplaces now covered by health and safety legislation. At first, this detail has had to be provided by pre-1974 provisions in statutes (*e.g.* the Factories Act 1961) and accompanying orders and regulations, but now these are being repealed and replaced by a more flexible and co-ordinated body of legislation enacted under powers delegated by Parliament in HASAWA to the Minister for Employment. So gradually there is emerging a more unified overall system of control of health and safety at work which depends on a hierarchy of four different forms of legislation. Since safety representatives involve all of them, it is necessary to understand their distinctive features.

(i) *The "Enabling Act"*

The overall "Enabling Act" is HASAWA. In addition to imposing duties on employers, it gives powers to various people, including the Minister for Employment. He may (among other things) make health and safety regulations "for any of the statute's general purposes" including, more specifically, for the appointment by recognised trade unions of safety representatives to represent employees in consultation with employers, and to have such other functions as may be set out in regulations (see ss. 2 (4) and 15).

(ii) *Regulations*

Regulations made by the Minister may repeal or modify the pre-1974 legislation and regulations made subsequently; they may confer powers (for example, on local authorities); they may impose criminal penalties or exclude or limit the possibility of criminal penalties. Breach of regulations gives a person who suffers loss or injury as a result a right to sue for damages in a civil action unless the specific regulation prohibits such right of action.

However, the Regulations which cover safety representatives and safety committees (subsequently referred to as "the Regulations" or "Regs.") do not impose criminal penalties nor do they give a *general* right to damages. This is not spelt out but depends on the nature of the rights and powers given. Indeed, the whole emphasis of the Regulations is that differences should be settled by existing and agreed industrial relations machinery. Only in the cases of refusal to allow a safety representative time off for his duties, or to pay him during his time off, is there provided the possibility of complaint to an industrial tribunal (see Chap. 3).

So by regulations the Minister has wide and flexible powers to make law and a speedy means of keeping the law in line with new circumstances. Also, regulations can take account of specific hazards or specific industries (*e.g.* the Power Press Regulations or the Ship Building and Ship Repairing Regulations). Nevertheless, as laws of the land, regulations' precise and often technical language is not always easy to understand, nor do they show how a regulation may best be complied with in practice. Since health and safety regulations must frequently apply to workplaces differing widely in size, age, layout, etc., the actual operation of a specific regulation may cause uncertainty; yet any infringement of its provisions may incur liability to damages or to criminal prosecution.

(iii) *Codes of Practice*

To provide practical guidance, HASAWA gives powers to the Health and Safety Commission to issue codes of practice to amplify the general duties in HASAWA or the regulations. So, for example, the Regulations are accompanied by a code of practice ("the Code") to provide practical guidance on the way in which safety representatives should actually operate.

Failure to observe the provisions of a code is not of itself either a criminal offence or grounds for a civil action for damages; its effect is similar to a breach of the Highway Code. First, any relevant provision of a code is admissible in evidence in legal proceedings; and secondly, a failure to observe a provision of a code relevant to the prosecution's case in any proceedings is taken to be proved unless the court is satisfied that the accused complied with the code's requirement or prohibition in some other acceptable way. So, despite their straightforward language, codes of practice have definite legal effects.

Nevertheless, the Regulations and the Code provide merely a basic framework. More detailed agreements can be negotiated on top of this framework by collective bargaining. So where the application of the law is unclear, or where differences are likely between management and workers, agreements should be negotiated to iron out and anticipate potential points of dispute, thereby avoiding the possibly serious consequences of argument just when an urgent issue of health or safety occurs.

(iv) *Guidance Notes*

As a supplement to the Regulations and the Code, the HSC has also issued a set of guidance notes ("the Guidance Notes" or "GN") to spell out more fully the implications of the legislation.

Such notes have no official status, but their advice must frequently go far to establish, say, that a particular procedure for safety representatives' workplace inspections conforms with good practice.

Note: the Regulations, the Code and the Guidance Notes have been issued by HMSO in one booklet, price 35p, showing the relevant portions of the Code and Guidance Notes set against the individual Regulation to which they relate. Readers may find access to the booklet useful in view of this book's frequent references to its contents.

The Health and Safety Commission, the Health and Safety Executive, and Advisory Committees

To co-ordinate and unify the administration of occupational health and safety formerly divided between a number of different government departments, HASAWA established a Health and Safety Commission ("HSC"). This is a governmental agency ultimately responsible to the Minister of Employment, with the general duty to promote compliance with HASAWA. Under a full-time chairman (currently Bill Simpson), it has three members nominated by each of the TUC and the CBI, two members nominated by local authorities, and one independent member. The HSC holds inquiries into accidents, and gives advice and information (*e.g.* by publications including guidance notes); it conducts and sponsors research, issues and approves codes of practice, and submits proposals to the Minister for new regulations.

Under the general control of the HSC is the Health and Safety Executive ("HSE") which, on a day-to-day basis, carries out the technical work of the HSC, *e.g.* by holding inquiries or drafting regulations. The HSE embraces the research bodies set up under previous legislation, and the previously separate inspectorates covering factories, mines and quarries, alkali and clean air, explosives and nuclear installations. So now it offers a comprehensive enforcement service which can be more rationally organised on a regional basis, with each office having experts, as required, to call upon.

Other inspectors are provided by local authorities' "environmental health officers" who traditionally have enforced such legislation as the Offices, Shops and Railway Premises Act 1963. Since 1977 they also enforce provisions of HASAWA in those premises where they were previously enforcing the 1963 Act, as well as some additional related activities. The long-term plan is that gradually local authorities will take over responsibility for the "new entrants" (see p. 4).

The HSC is also establishing 18 advisory committees either for certain subjects (*e.g.* major hazards, dangerous substances, toxic substances) or specific industries (*e.g.* agriculture, construction, ceramics). Each committee has representatives from unions, employers, and the HSE, and many include local authority representatives and outside experts. So this is another level at which unions are involved in administration and policy-making under HASAWA.

The Employment Medical Advisory Service

The Employment Medical Advisory Service ("EMAS") provides information, advice, research staff and facilities to the HSC, HSE and inspectors, as well as to employers and unions, relating to the health of employed persons and health hazards. EMAS is organised around regional offices (see Chap. 7) and consists of about 140 full-time doctors and nurses, working under the umbrella of the HSC, studying the medical requirements of different jobs, carrying out medical surveys, and conducting periodic examinations of workers' exposure to hazards. An Employment Medical Adviser can demand that an employer allows him the opportunity at any reasonable time during working hours to examine any worker whose health he believes is affected by his work.

Enforcement

HASAWA's emphasis on preventive measures is reflected in new powers whereby an inspector, who considers someone to have contravened the Act or a regulation, may serve an *improvement notice* requiring the matter to be remedied by a certain date. This date must not be earlier than six weeks subsequent to the notice (so that within this time the recipient may exercise his right to appeal against it to an industrial tribunal), and should give a reasonable length of time within which the matter can be put right. The effect of bringing an appeal is to suspend the operation of the notice until either the tribunal cancels or confirms the notice. Both the recipient of the notice and the inspector may appeal against the tribunal's decision, first to the Employment Appeal Tribunal, then to the Court of Appeal, and finally to the House of Lords sitting as a court. However, such appeals can only be pursued on questions of law, *i.e.* on questions as to the application of the correct law to the facts. Appeals are relatively rare, however, and improvement notices are viewed as the mildest legal back-up to the inspector's normal reliance on persuasion and advice.

If an inspector considers a person's activities both contravene a statutory provision and involve now or in the future the risk of serious personal injury, he may serve a *prohibition notice* directing that the recipient cease the activities complained of unless the matters specified in the notice are put right. If the risk of personal injury is imminent, the notice can take effect immediately; otherwise it can specify the period within which the matters must be remedied. In either case, the recipient can appeal in the same way as for improvement notices, but the operation of a notice is only suspended if a tribunal agrees to the recipient's application. Often the prohibition notice will be served after a recipient's failure to comply with an improvement notice.

The remaining enforcement powers of inspectors resemble those under the pre-1974 legislation: depending on the nature of the offence, a person or undertaking, including an officer of such undertaking (but currently *not* the Crown), may be liable to be fined up to a maximum at present standing at £1,000 by a magistrates' court, or be fined and/or imprisoned for a maximum two years by the Crown Court. This more serious alternative is specifically stated to be available against those failing to comply with a prohibition notice. Also inspectors have extended powers under HASAWA, s. 20, to enter premises with or without the police or an authorised expert (*e.g.* the public analyst); to examine and investigate premises, for which purpose inspectors may require workplaces to be left undisturbed; to take measurements, recordings, photographs and samples; to require information from anyone, as well as books and documents, and any necessary facilities or assistance; to dismantle or test any dangerous article or substance and render harmless anything which they may believe is a cause of imminent danger of serious personal injury.

2 The Appointment of Safety Representatives

HASAWA and the Regulations state simply that a recognised trade union may appoint safety representatives to represent their fellow employees. So employers have no legal right to be involved in the process of appointment. Nevertheless, a union must take into account a number of practical considerations when considering appointments, and these may point to the wisdom of consultation with employers. So, notwithstanding unions' unilateral right to appoint whom they choose, unions in practice may often agree with employers the extent of safety representatives' constituencies, the duration of their term of office, and suchlike. Trade unions appointing safety representatives must also observe certain requirements in the Regulations, some of which raise questions of wider employment law.

Appointment by a trade union

A preliminary point is that the appointment of safety representatives must be made in accordance with any relevant union rule. Union rules are most obviously found in rulebooks but they may also stem from

> "custom and practice, by procedures which have developed over the years and which, although well understood by those who operate them, are not formally set out in the rules."

Not all rulebooks mention such important part-time officials as shop stewards, and even fewer rulebooks mention safety representatives; yet clearly a practice has already developed, often evidenced in unions' handbooks, regarding the appointment of representatives by individual unions. In many cases safety representatives are elected by the workmates they are to represent; alternatively, the appointment is made by those representing the union on a shop stewards' or joint negotiating committee. These "shop-floor" elections or selections will then normally have to be approved or ratified by the relevant committee of the union.

It is important to observe any union rules concerning the appointment of safety representatives to avoid the possibility that a representative's appointment may be called in question either by fellow-members or (possibly) by the employer. Failure to comply with the rules could lead to the setting aside of the appointment by the union's own committees or the courts. Difficulties raised by an employer with regard to a defective appointment are likely to lead to industrial relations problems. If they ultimately take the form of the employer refusing the alleged safety representative time-off in which to carry out his duties or undertake training, the representative may make a complaint to an industrial tribunal (see p. 41) and the tribunal may in effect decide the validity of the appointment.

The union making the appointment must be "recognised" for the purpose of collective bargaining (Reg. 3 (1))

This requirement raises some technical points of law, which need to be discussed separately (see, for a fuller discussion, *Trade Unions* by Richard Kidner, in this series).

The union in question must satisfy the statutory definition (TULRA, s. 28) of a trade union, that is, it must (a) consist wholly or mainly of "workers," and (b) be an organisation whose principal purposes include the regulation of relations between such workers and employers (or employers' associations). These definitions are sufficiently wide to cause little difficulty: conventional trade unions primarily exist to regulate relations between their members and employers, as do many other professional organisations and staff associations; and "workers" covers those in work or seeking work and even the self-employed.

To be recognised, a union must also be independent (Reg. 2 (1)). This means that the union must not be under the domination or control of an employer *and* not be *liable* to interference by an employer arising out of the provision of financial or material support or by any other means whatsoever tending towards such control (TULRA, s. 30 (1)). Most unions already have "certificates of independence" issued by an official called the Certification Officer, and these are then conclusive evidence in all court proceedings of the union's status. It is, however, worth noting that the courts have recently confirmed that "liable" means vulnerable to possible interference in the future rather than subject to actual or probable interference.

Failure to satisfy either the requirement of independence or the definition of a trade union does not of itself prevent an organisation and an employer agreeing to the appointment of "voluntary" safety representatives. However, such representatives will not be safety representatives for the purposes of the Regulations; so any rights they enjoy will entirely depend on the agreement struck with the employer (see below).

"Collective bargaining" is also statutorily defined (EPA, s. 126 (1)): it means negotiations relating to a list of matters which include all the most obvious bargainable topics, *i.e.*:

terms and conditions of workers;
the physical conditions in which workers are required to work;
the engagement or non-engagement of workers;
termination or suspension of employment;
allocation of work between workers;
matters of discipline;
membership or non-membership of a union;
facilities for union officials;
machinery for negotiation and other procedures relating to any of the previous matters including recognition.

So for a union to be entitled to appoint a safety representative, it must negotiate with the relevant employer on one or more of the above matters: it will then be said to be *recognised* by such employer. If it negotiates on matters which are not on the list (*e.g.* sub-contracting work), then such negotiations do not in law amount to collective bargaining, and the union cannot be said to be recognised for the purpose of the Regulations.

Usually, it is easy to tell whether a union is recognised if, for example, the union negotiates its members' rates of pay, hours of work and entitlement to holidays, or represents them individually or collectively over disciplinary questions. Nevertheless, cases do occur where it is unclear whether a union has been recognised. In these circumstances, the courts have said that for there to be recognition, some degree of mutuality must be shown so that, on the one hand, the employer (or his properly authorised representative, who might be a safety officer) acknowledges the union for the relevant purpose, while on the other hand the union, by its duly authorised official, assents to that acknowledgement. Any such agreement need not be formal or in writing, and can be inferred from the conduct of the parties provided that there exists some clear and unambiguous evidence of agreement, normally taking the form of conduct over a period of time.

This emphasises two points: (a) employers must inform any management representatives involved in discussions with workers of the extent of their authority, and the undertakings's policy regarding union recognition. If it is opposed to recognition, care must be taken as to the way issues are discussed with workers' representatives, particularly in consultative committees where it is easy for discussion to slide into negotiation; (b) recognition "to any extent" is sufficient. So the grant of negotiating rights relating merely to one of the listed bargainable topics suffices even though such negotiating rights may be unconnected with health and safety; also a union can be "recognised" in respect of just one worker in a workforce. So permitting a union official to represent a worker in disciplinary proceedings or workers of a certain level of seniority or of a certain description may constitute recognition. Consequently, the right to appoint safety representatives is quite unconnected with the size of a workplace or the number of trade union members.

Where unions are recognised for only a minority of workers, they will probably leap at the chance to represent not merely their existing members but also the (presumably) similar health and safety interests of all their non-unionised workmates, thereby affording them a demonstration of the benefits of union membership.

Most unions rely on their own efforts to gain recognition, but ACAS can on its own initiative or at the union's or employer's request offer conciliation, arbitration or advice with regard to a recognition dispute. In practice, both unions and employers usually prefer to rely on their own unaided efforts to settle disputes over recognition, and nothing in the Regulations or the EPA makes the use of industrial action unlawful. However, where the recognition dispute is between unions affiliated to the TUC, they should first resort to the TUC's own disputes procedures.

The position of non-unionised workers or members of a non-recognised union, etc.

If a recognised union refuses to act on behalf of non-members or of members of a non-recognised union or if members of a recognised union choose not to appoint a safety representative, such workers are still entitled to be consulted and receive information under the employer's general duty (HASAWA, s. 2 (2) (*c*)) to provide all employees with "such information, instruction, training and supervision as is necessary to ensure, so far as is reasonably practicable, the health and safety at work of his employees." Implicit in the employer's general duties to provide safe systems of work, and safe storage and transport of substances, etc., is also a duty, where necessary, to consult employees affected.

In practice, independently of HASAWA, many employers, whatever the union status of their workers, consult individual employees, who speak for their workmates in the workplace as "voluntary" safety representatives, or carry on consultations through safety committees. Such arrangements frequently continue perfectly satisfactorily, notwithstanding the operation since October 1978 of the Regulations; alternatively, such arrangements can now be put on a statutory footing if the recognised trade union or unions so require (see also Chap. 6). A further possibility may be for safety representatives to be appointed jointly by union and non-union members.

The real difficulty for non-recognised work groups or non-unionised employees is that they have little scope for securing compliance with HASAWA or the Regulations otherwise than by recourse to the inspectorate, whereas recognised unions can back up their members' interest in health and safety by collective bargaining. Nor, of course, do voluntary representatives have any statutory rights to time off (see p. 33).

Safety representatives are appointable from among the employees of the employer and must normally work with their constituents

The Regulations assume a close identity of interest between safety representatives and their constituents. Normally a safety representative must himself be a member of the workplace he represents. So Regulation 3 (3) (*b*) requires that a person ceases to be a safety representative when he ceases to be employed at the workplace for which he was appointed unless he represents more than one workplace in which case his appointment continues while he remains employed at any one of these workplaces (see p. 24). This indicates that representation should be tied to a particular shop, section or department within an undertaking, rather than to the whole establishment of which these form part; and this is confirmed by the definition of workplace: this provides that in relation to a safety representative a workplace means "any place or places where the group or groups of employees he is appointed to represent are likely to work . . ." (Reg. 2).

Guidance Note 6 explains the relationship of a representative to his constituents further; unions will "normally appoint representatives to represent a group or groups of workers of a class for which the union has negotiating rights." So it is assumed that safety representatives, as union appointees, will represent existing bargaining groups which will normally tally with the bargaining groups represented by shop stewards. It is also possible that safety representatives may represent by mutual agreement between appropriate unions more than one union's members, for example, in a small workplace where the number of recognised trade unions is high, and hence the potential number of safety representatives that *could* be appointed is large relative to the total numbers employed. Also linking representation to particular groups does not preclude the representative from raising with the employer general matters affecting the health and safety of employees as a whole, whether or not unionised (GN 6 and 7).

Other cases where representatives' constituencies need not be linked to their own work groups are, for instance, where there are rapidly changing conditions including changes in the levels of manpower (*e.g.* in docks, shipbuilding and construction sites), or in workplaces where most workers go out to work (*e.g.* goods or freight depots, builders' yards and service depots of all kinds). The principle of appointing representatives by reference to workplaces may also have to be modified where there is a wide variety of work going on in one location, involving very different skills and hazards, and hence requiring differently specialised safety representatives if they are adequately to represent their workmates. Similar considerations apply in workplaces with especially high levels of risks (*e.g.* construction sites, chemical works, and some research establishments) or sites which have high risks at particular stages (*e.g.* demolition sites, excavation, etc.) or where most employees are engaged in low risk activities but where one or two processes or activities or machines involve specially high levels of risk (GN 9). By contrast, Reg. 8 specifically exempts representatives appointed by Equity or the Musicians' Union from having even to be employees of the employer. Regulation 3 (1) similarly excepts the long-standing case of non-employee workmen's inspectors under the Mines and Quarries Act 1954. These numerous exceptions emphasise the need to apply the Regulations flexibly to meet the varying circumstances of different workplaces.

Numbers of safety representatives to appoint

Since the right to appoint safety representatives belongs solely to recognised trade unions, theoretically such unions are free to appoint as many representatives as they please. However, there must be a limit on the number of representatives that can effectively do the job, quite apart from the frequent difficulty of finding volunteers for union office, and especially for such posts as safety representatives where knowledge and experience, possibly to a highly specialist degree, may be necessary. Also other recognised unions in that workplace may seek to appoint representatives. If there is the necessary goodwill and identity of interest between different unions, it is of course sensible to have one representative acting jointly on behalf of all trade unionists. Otherwise the appointment by one union of its own safety representatives may provoke pressure from the employer on operational grounds to reduce the number of representatives that another union may seek to appoint.

Employers will be unhappy if more representatives are appointed than they consider necessary since not only will such representatives be entitled to the additional statutory protection against transfer and dismissal (see p. 25) but they are (see p. 33) also entitled to paid time-off during the discharge of their union duties. If an excessive number of representatives are appointed, this can interfere with an employer's operational requirements of running his business; so employers will often prefer that shop stewards act as safety representatives (see p. 21) or that in multi-union workplaces one representative acts for a number of unions. The absence of representatives from their normal work may be unpopular, too, with their workmates if, for example, this affects the output of a group whose pay is wholly or partially determined by their collective productivity.

Equally, the appointment of too few representatives can result in the incomplete coverage of a workplace and the inadequate representation and protection of their constituents' interests. This especially applies where there is a high level of risks, a widely dispersed workforce or risks requiring local or specialised skills and knowledge, most particularly where the hazards vary as between different categories of workers within a group. Shift work also increases the number of representatives required since more than one representative needs to be available during each shift to experience the conditions of work for himself and to be available to speak with his constituents.

The correct number of representatives for any one workplace, therefore, is dependent on a number of different factors. Some of these, set out in Guidance Note 9, have already been mentioned on p. 18, others are mentioned in Guidance Note 8, and include the total number of employees, the size of the workplace, the variety of different occupations and of workplace locations, the operation of shift systems, the type of work activity, and the degree and character of the inherent dangers of the work, any of which may affect what is an appropriate number of representatives for a particular workplace.

Finally the criterion of the right number must be the number needed to carry out the function of safety representation effectively in any workplace. Often the pattern with regard to safety representatives can follow closely the pattern already established for shop stewards both as to their number and the workgroups they represent (see p. 17). This may mean (see p. 21) that the shop steward and safety representative is one and the same person. Alternatively, it may be necessary to ignore existing industrial relations groupings and appoint safety representatives solely by reference to groups of workers with similar health and safety problems. Once again flexibility in applying the Regulations must be the keynote.

Qualifications for safety representatives

The Regulations require that safety representatives should normally have had so far as is reasonably practicable two years' previous employment with that employer, or at least two years' experience in similar employment (Reg. 3 (4)). This is clearly intended to ensure that the representative has the necessary understanding of the employer's undertaking so that, for instance, he appreciates the industrial relations background against which he must work. However, he is not required to have spent those two years in the workplace he represents although in practice this may well be a desirable additional qualification and may be something which the appointing union may require when making appointments. If a union agrees such a provision or a requirement of a minimum age qualification (*e.g.* 21) with an employer, the union to this extent is limiting the freedom granted by the Regulations to appoint whom it chooses.

Alternatively, two years' experience in similar employment will be helpful, with such a representative's fresh outlook counterbalancing his lack of experience of his new employer's undertaking. Guidance Note 10 gives examples of cases where it may not be reasonably practicable to require representatives to have two years' qualifying experience, for example, where the employer or workplace site is newly established or where work is of short duration or where there is a high labour turnover; also this requirement does not apply to musicians or actors (see p. 18) since they may be represented by full-time union officials who may well not have any experience within the profession or employment.

Shop stewards as safety representatives: pros and cons

Unions have differed over whether they should appoint shop stewards as safety representatives. Much depends on whether the main consideration is to integrate health and safety into the existing industrial relations and collective bargaining set-up (in which case there must clearly be advantages in the appointment of existing shop stewards); whether the particular workplace's hazards require a representative with specialised knowledge of health and safety (in which case the appointment of such a specialist will be preferable) or, if no such employee exists, then a suitably interested person should be appointed who can with training and experience develop the necessary expertise.

In favour of the appointment of shop stewards is their pre-existing relationships with the employer, with their own members, and with their full-time union officials; also in a multi-union workplace, they will usually already have contacts with other union representatives. Employers may also prefer the appointment of shop stewards since it avoids providing a possibly duplicated set of facilities and paid time off to another union official (see Chap. 3); however, if every steward is to be a safety representative, it may lead (in the employer's eyes) to the appointment of an excessive number of representatives even though it will certainly reduce the total number of union officials overall.

Where separate safety representatives are appointed they need to be integrated into existing collective bargaining systems (*e.g.* as regards, at least, access to shop steward committees and joint negotiating committees) and to be accorded equal status with shop stewards by both unions and employers. Otherwise health and safety is likely to continue as a "Cinderella topic" in the eyes of workers and management, with safety representatives denied the wide-ranging support they may need to back up effective bargaining.

The difficulty of achieving this degree of integration without creating organisational overlaps or conflicts is, of course, one of the attractions of appointing stewards as safety representatives. Given a steward's experience, health and safety is more likely to be regarded as a bargainable issue—as the Regulations assume it to be (see p. 28)—always provided that shop stewards can effectively carry the increased workload. This will be advantageous for those unions and employers who may be unfamiliar with safety representatives and their functions. One way of spreading the load for already burdened shop stewards is for certain stewards to take a specialist interest in health and safety. Other stewards can then consult them on points of difficulty. This specialisation may go further, so that the health and safety stewards take over responsibility for such matters, provided that management will co-operate to ignore the Regulation's requirement of the close link needed between workplace employees and representatives (see p. 17). A further solution may be to appoint safety representatives not from shop stewards but from former part-time officials or members with negotiating experience.

A disadvantage, however, of doubling up safety and health and industrial relations responsibilities is that disagreements in one area can taint relations in the other. Clearly, specialist representatives are needed in workplaces with high or specialised health and safety risks or where there is a widely spread workforce. Indeed, in certain workplaces this can be an argument in favour of appointing full-time safety representatives who will provide the advantage of continuity; they will also need diminishing amounts of time off for training as they gain the necessary skills and specialised knowledge. Moreover, their employers, unions, and constituents have the advantage of more consistent representation. Counter-balancing disadvantages, however, are the possible remoteness of full-time officials from their constituents and the risk of apathy from over-familiarity with problems. In the last resort as important as specialist knowledge and expertise may be a plain man's down-to-earth approach, with a good sense of priorities and of the practical implications of expert advice.

Notification of the employer

Once a safety representative has been appointed, his union must notify the employer in writing of his name and the group or groups of employees whom he represents, whereupon the representative can then exercise his statutory functions (Reg. 3 (2)). Especially where safety representatives are being appointed for the first time, there should be previous consultation with the employer so that notification of a representative's name does not come as a bolt out of the blue and thereby provide the cause of an avoidable dispute. Consultations with the employer are particularly necessary where a number of representatives are appointed with possible implications for the employer's operational requirements, or where, because of the dispersed or hazardous nature of the workplace, representatives may require large amounts of time off or where the union wishes to depart from recommendations in the Regulations or Guidance Notes. Nevertheless, in the last resort the union does have the right to appoint whom it chooses.

An employer may reasonably require safety representatives to carry credentials, signed by the union or section of it which ratifies his appointment, and (possibly) counter-signed by the employer. Representatives may also be required to wear identifying badges, which may be as useful to their workmates as to management. Indeed, in large workplaces unions should ensure that the name and location of newly appointed safety representatives are passed on to all their constituents, as well as to other union officials in the undertaking and to full time district officials.

Additionally it is worth notifying appointments to the offices of the local HSE inspectorate and of any relevant local authority inspector, since not only are good working relationships with inspectors of great assistance to representatives but inspectors are under a duty in certain circumstances to pass on information to safety representatives (see Chap.4).

Termination of appointment

Regulation 3 (3) provides three ways in which persons may cease to be safety representatives:

(a) The simplest method is resignation. As with appointments (see p. 12), resignations of trade union officials must comply with any union rules that may regulate such matters. Also it seems advisable to ensure that the resignation takes effect at the same time as the employer is notified, exactly as Regulation 3 (2) requires in the case of appointments (see p. 23).

(b) Similarly removal by the union must be in accordance with the union and common law rules governing termination of the office of safety representatives or of union officials in general. Failure to comply with such rules can have two consequences: (1) the safety representative remains in office, and this may lead to conflict and confusion between him and any replacement that the union may have sought to appoint in his stead; (2) a safety representative removed contrary to these rules can sue in the courts for a declaration that his removal is of no effect, and for damages for the union's failure to observe the terms of the contract which the union rules comprise with him as a union member.

The likeliest cause of complaint in the removal of an official is a failure to observe either a procedural requirement of the union rules themselves or the so-called common law rules of "natural justice": these are rules read into such appointments by the courts so that those removing a representative from office are, for instance, obliged to give him the reasons for his removal, the opportunity to prepare and argue his case, and to do so before an unbiased union committee. In practice, however, even if the courts decide in the representative's favour, the long-term consequences are normally minimal since the union, by removing him a second time in compliance with its rules and the rules of natural justice can do so perfectly lawfully, thereby depriving the removed representative of any further remedy. This means that any damages for wrongful removal in the first instance are likely to be small. On the other hand, court proceedings are expensive and time-consuming and may disrupt a union's good internal relations besides often creating adverse publicity.

(c) Removal as a result of a representative's transfer from his workplace or outright dismissal from his employment. If there is any question that such actions may be viewed as victimisation of a union official, they require the same careful handling that the transfer or dismissal of a shop steward demands. The ACAS Code of Practice on Disciplinary Practice and Procedure states:

> "Although normal disciplinary standards should apply to trade union officials' conduct as employees, no disciplinary action beyond an oral warning should be taken until the circumstances of the case have been discussed with a senior trade union representative or full-time official" (Para. 15 (*b*)).

Strangely, no mention of these matters is made in the Regulations, Code or Guidance Notes. However, as union officials and members participating in the activities of an *independent* union, safety representatives also have the following special protection under provisions of EPCA 1978, which are more fully described in the Law at Work titles *Union Members* and *Trade Unions*.

(i) *Transfers from the workplace*

Transfer from the workplace or any other discriminatory conduct (*e.g.* loss of overtime) taken against a representative on grounds of his union activities constitute action short of dismissal (EPCA, ss. 23-26). If such action is held to be well-founded by an industrial tribunal the representative is entitled to compensation from the employer. Significantly, nothing in EPCA will enable the representative to be transferred back to his former workplace, so if that is what he wants, he will have to rely on any pressure the union can bring to bear on the employer.

(ii) *Dismissals from employment*

Dismissals from employment for union activities may also be the subject of complaint to an industrial tribunal (EPCA, s. 58

(1)). The representative must prove both that he was dismissed because of his union activities, in which case the dismissal is automatically unfair as being for an "inadmissible reason." (This exempts him from having to satisfy the normal prerequisites for an unfair dismissal action of 52 weeks prior continuous employment with that employer and an age below normal retiring age (EPCA, s. 64 (3) as amended).)

The remedies available to the representative will be reinstatement in his old job, re-engagement in an equivalent job or compensation. In the case of the first two remedies, the representative must opt for one of these remedies, and it must also be practicable for the employer to effect such remedy (EPCA, ss. 68-70).

(iii) *Interim relief*

Interim relief for representatives dismissed for union activities is available if within seven days of the termination of his employment, the representative makes a complaint of unfair dismissal to an industrial tribunal (ECPA, ss. 77-79). The complaint must be accompanied by a written certificate from an authorised official of an *independent* trade union giving reasonable grounds for supposing that the representative was dismissed because of his union activities. If a tribunal then makes a preliminary finding that on a full hearing of the complaint it is likely that he will be found to have been unfairly dismissed for his union activities, the representative is entitled pending the full hearing to reinstatement, re-engagement or the (notional) continuation of his contract of employment, *i.e.* for the purposes *only* of pay, pension rights, seniority, etc. If the employer fails to comply with a reinstatement or re-engagement order, the tribunal will "continue" the representative's contract of employment *and* order compensation; if the employer fails to pay money due under a continued contract such sum will be payable separately if the tribunal decides at the full hearing that the representative was unfairly dismissed; failure to continue the contract in other respects entitles the representative to compensation.

Ultimately, all the above remedies are likely to end up as orders for compensation since this is by far the most common remedy awarded and, in the usually strained circumstances under which a representative is removed by an employer, it is probably all that is practicable. So if the representative is dissatisfied with compensation, he will have to negotiate for the restoration of his job through an existing grievance or disputes procedure or simply by ad hoc bargaining. Alternatively, a representative may seek to rely on such industrial pressure as he or his union can command.

Disputes

Many of the matters discussed in this chapter give rise to possible disputes between unions and employers, workers and their employers or unions, or among unions. The Regulations stress that disputes should be settled by "the existing agreed industrial relations machinery," and (with the exception of refusal of time off or pay for time off—see p. 41) *not* by the courts or industrial tribunals. In short, the Regulations build on existing structures of collective bargaining *including* existing disputes procedures. Only where all internal disputes procedures and possibilities of external conciliation by joint industrial bodies or ACAS have been exhausted may enforcement through the courts be appropriate. This may take one of two forms: either a complaint brought by a safety representative before an industrial tribunal for time-off (see Chap. 3), as a means of testing, say, an employer's refusal to recognise a union's appointee as safety representative; or, as a last resort, the inspectorate itself may initiate action initially by serving an improvement notice, and finally, if events so justify, by prosecuting an employer for breach of his duties under HASAWA (see p. 10).

3 The Role and Status of Safety Representatives

Safety representatives and collective bargaining

Safety representatives are new figures on the collective bargaining scene. Yet under the general duties in HASAWA all that is mentioned rather vaguely is the employer's duty to consult with representatives who shall represent the employees "with a view to the making and maintenance of arrangements which will enable the employer and his employees to co-operate effectively in promoting and developing measures to ensure the health and safety at work of the employees and in checking the effectiveness of such measures" (s. 2 (4), (6)).

However, HASAWA also provides that representatives shall have such other functions as may be prescribed by regulations. These are set out in Regulation 4 in some detail (see Chaps. 4-6) but it is still too soon after the Regulations first came into effect for much practice to have accumulated around this bare statutory framework: so inevitably this discussion of safety representatives' role and status (and of their functions) is largely based on the Regulations, Code and Guidance Notes, and particularly the way they relate to each other.

None of these documents specifically mentions collective bargaining. The Regulations do give representatives positive powers of representation on behalf of their workmates (Reg. 4 (1) (*c*) and (*d*). See Chap. 4); and the Code speaks of "encouraging co-operation between employer and his employees" and representatives bringing to employers' notice unsafe or unhealthy conditions, etc. (para. 5). The only clear indication that health and safety is to be the subject of bargaining comes from reading the full range of safety representatives' rights in the Regulations, Code and Guidance Notes as a whole. Also, it is clear from the bargaining between the TUC and the CBI over the contents of the Regulations before their enactment, that unions certainly envisaged a negotiating role for safety representatives which will now not readily be conceded.

From some agreements negotiated at the time that the Regulations came into operation, it seems that their potential for extending the range of bargaining has not been appreciated—or, if appreciated, it has deliberately been negated by continuing to treat representatives as mere participants in a consultative process, entitled to make representations which the employer is equally free to reject. Trade unionists should therefore look critically at agreements they negotiate to ensure that they do not accept limitations on safety representatives' powers (*e.g.* the occasions when they may carry out investigations and the people they may consult) even though in the last resort no agreement can limit a representative's statutory rights.

The role of a full participant in collective bargaining at workplace level has important consequences for a safety representative's status, both in relation to his union and to his employer, which need to be considered in turn. Not surprisingly, (as already mentioned) the full implications of such a status are not yet universally accepted. In practice, much depends on particular workplaces and circumstances. This book generally seeks to explain the position assuming the full realisation of the Regulations' potential.

Safety representatives' status as trade union officials

The powers of a union's officers and full-time officials depend on the rules contained in the union's rulebooks. Few rulebooks, however, mention shop stewards or safety representatives but there is judicial authority for the view that a union's custom and practice may also be a source of its rules (see p. 12). Clearly most shop stewards' activities fall into sufficiently well-established patterns to satisfy such a test, and this must now also be the case in most unions with respect to safety representatives. So by these means authority is also conferred by the union on these part-time officials.

Nevertheless the treatment of shop stewards and safety representatives in rulebooks does reveal the difficulty of incorporating part-time officials neatly into union structures when they depend for their appointment and effectiveness on their workplace constituents. In practice, this means that stewards and representatives will often be quite as sensitive to the attitudes of their constituents with whom they work as to the central authority of their union; and this may create tensions with full-time local officials whose sole authority comes centrally from the union. On the other hand, part-time officials also need the benefit of full-time officials' contact with the wider union organisation and their information and experience about other establishments in which the union has members and safety representatives (see Chap. 4). So safety representatives must try to maintain simultaneously their loyalties to their constituents and good relations with their local full-time officials.

Safety representatives' status as negotiators with employers

Even when the safety representative is accepted as a negotiator in the full collective bargaining sense, there remains some uncertainty about the nature of his role: is his function to regulate *with* the employer adequate standards of health and safety arrived at jointly by the process of bargaining; or is it the more limited "policing" role of checking that management observes its primary duties of ensuring health and safety in the workplace?

The Regulations, Code and Guidance Notes do not provide answers to these questions, and in practice the position is probably that individual representatives follow their own line or that of their unions or constituencies in deciding the degree to which they *collaborate* with management over health and safety. In either case, if the role of the safety representative is to be more than a consultative one, he must maintain good contacts with management and, at the same time, a genuine degree of independence from management in order to retain the respect of both his constituents and the managers with whom he must negotiate. This will be especially true both in the early years of these Regulations and also subsequently in the case of newly appointed representatives as they work out the ambit of their duties and establish relations with their constituents. Early in his appointment it may be uncertain to what extent his workmates will support a safety representative's initiatives—yet without such support his demands must lose effectiveness. Also, without independence from management, a safety representative loses his value *to the employer* as a new channel of communication with the workforce, which forms such an important part of his role (see Chap. 4).

The legal liability of safety representatives

Reg. 4 (1) states that no function conferred by the Regulations shall be regarded as imposing any legal duty on safety representatives over and above those statutory and common law obligations imposed on him in common with all employees (*i.e.* to take reasonable care of himself and of others who may be affected by his acts or omissions at work; to co-operate so as to enable his employer to comply with or perform any statutory obligation; and not to interfere or misuse intentionally or recklessly anything provided under any statutory requirement for health, safety or welfare purposes) HASAWA, ss. 7 and 8). Also a safety representative, by accepting or not objecting to a course of action taken or proposed by the employer in regard to some health or safety hazard, does not incur any legal responsibility for that action. Further, the HSC have directed that the inspectorate should not prosecute a safety representative for any act or omission in the performance of his statutory functions (GN 11); and some unions go further and suggest that employers should indemnify safety representatives against any liability that could, as the result of an unforeseen loophole in the Code or Regulations, render a representative liable for something done in the course of his duties.

However, a point not dealt with by the Regulations is the effect of a safety representative's approval, say, of a new manufacturing process which is subsequently the cause of a constituent's injury. In response to the worker's claim for common law damages, the employer could put forward the defence that he had done everything reasonably practicable to make the process safe, and as evidence the employer might well cite the safety representative's approval.

A safety representative's approval, however, will be only one of the factors reviewed by a court in assessing the reasonableness of the employer's conduct, and the representative's experience and expertise in regard to that issue will be relevant. Nevertheless, a safety representative should generally express his approval cautiously and, if in writing, with any relevant qualifications of the circumstances in which it is given, *e.g.* the then extent of his (and others') experience and expertise, his opportunities for inspection, the foreseeability of injuries, etc. Arguably, approval should not be expressed in writing at all since excessive reliance may be placed on it to the potential disadvantage of an injured fellow-employee. However, a totally non-committal response should be balanced against the adverse effect this is likely to have on relations with the employer. Whatever he does communicate to the employer should be accurately recorded for the representative's own benefit.

Also, the Regulations' exemption of safety representatives from liability might not affect a representative who has agreed with his employer, say, that all workers' complaints are to go to management only through the representative. If an employee's complaint of a dangerous machine is not passed on by his representative and the employee is injured due to its lack of repair, he could (if he so wished) sue the representative in a common law action for negligence, for his failure to carry out his duty. Nevertheless, the more obvious claims would still be against the employer for his breach of statutory duty and negligence in failing to maintain a safe system of work. The representative's failure to pass on the employee's complaint is unlikely to provide the employer with an adequate defence.

Facilities for safety representatives

Strangely, although the Regulations specify that such facilities and assistance must be afforded safety representatives when making inspections of the workplace as they may reasonably require (Regs. 5 (3) and 6 (2), see p. 62), there is no other mention of the provision of facilities for safety representatives. However, the ACAS Code on "Time Off for Trade Union Duties and Activities" (see below) which covers safety representatives, does say that management should make available "facilities necessary for officials to perform their duties efficiently and to communicate effectively with members, fellow lay officials and full-time officers" (para. 10).

Clearly just to provide a channel of communication with his constituents, his employer, his union and the inspectorate, a safety representative is likely to need secretarial and reprographic facilities, internal and external telephones, an office where he can talk to a constituent or inspector in confidence, a suitably placed notice board for his constituents, and a large room in which he can, when necessary, meet his constituents *en masse.* He will also need secure storage facilities for inspection, investigation and correspondence files, as well as for publications and health and safety literature generally. Additionally (see p. 62), he may need equipment for inspections. Many of these facilities are already available to shop stewards, and therefore management may jib at their duplication for safety representatives; so here is an advantage, at least to management, in the appointment of shop stewards as representatives. However, even where this is not done, many facilities can be conveniently shared by representative and shop steward.

Time off

In addition, the employer's active co-operation is essential to allow safety representatives time off during working hours to carry out their statutory functions and for training in the performance of such functions. In both cases the employer must permit such time off with pay as is *necessary* for these purposes (Reg. 4 (2)), but different codes of practice seek to explain the meaning of "necessary."

Time off for the statutory functions

The Code of Practice on Time Off for Trade Union Duties and Activities issued by ACAS reminds unionists when making arrangements for time off of such operational requirements as the particular demands in process industries of production and safety, or in any industry, whatever the size, of not fragmenting workforces. Equally, employers should be aware of officials' problems in representing constituents effectively and in maintaining communications, particularly where members work part-time or on shifts or in scattered workplaces or are married women with domestic commitments which limit the possibilities of participation in union affairs outside working hours. Unions and employers need to negotiate agreements appropriate to the particular circumstances of their workplace, although the absence of an agreement should not preclude the granting of time off.

EPCA, ss. 27 and 28 and the ACAS Code distinguish between *paid* time off for *officials'* industrial relations duties between the employer and their constituents, and *employees' unpaid* time off to take part in a recognised union's internal activities. Regulation 4 (2) merely speaks of *paid* time off for safety representatives as shall be *necessary* for the purposes of performing their functions (*i.e.* under HASAWA, s. 2 (4) and Reg. 4 (1)) whereas the "purposes" for which the ACAS Code, para. 13 recommends that reasonable *paid* time off should be permitted include:

(a) collective bargaining with the appropriate level of management;
(b) informing constituents about negotiations or consultations with management;
(c) *meeting with other lay officials or with full-time union officers on matters which are concerned with industrial relations between his employer and any associated employer and their employees;
(d) interviews with and on behalf of constituents on grievance and discipline matters concerning them and their employer;
(e) *appearing on behalf of constituents before an outside official body such as an industrial tribunal, which is dealing with an industrial relations matter concerning the employer; and
(f) *explaining to new employees whom he will represent the role of the union in the workplace industrial relations structure.

Those purposes marked with an asterisk are not covered by the specific functions listed in the Regulations (see Chap. 4) although they may fall within the wider (and vaguer) ambit of HASAWA. Nevertheless, provided that a request for time off comes within either the Regulations or EPCA, s. 27 and the ACAS Code, the applicant will be entitled to *paid* time off, and both permit the same procedure of complaints to industrial tribunals if time off is refused or if the official is not paid during his time off (see p. 41).

However, where safety representatives take time off for something not covered by either the Regulations or the ACAS Code, for example, to discuss a safety matter together before a statutory safety committee, this may not be "a matter concerned with industrial relations," in which case the safety representatives may be involved merely in union activities, and at best would only be entitled to *unpaid* time off. Even this is uncertain since the ACAS Code concedes that "there may be occasions when it is reasonable for unions to hold meetings of members during working hours because of the urgency of the matter to be discussed or where to do so would not adversely affect production or services" (para. 22). So if an industrial tribunal holds that neither the urgency of the matter nor the state of production justified representatives taking time off, an employer could regard a safety representative taking time off for such purposes as in breach of his contract of employment, giving rise possibly to grounds for his fair dismissal provided that, in making the dismissal, the employer complies with the necessary statutory requirements of EPCA, ss. 57 and 58 (1) and (2) (see the Law at Work title *Union Members*).

The ACAS Code, paras. 23-30, makes recommendations relating to all types of time off. Both management and unions should be aware of safety representatives' roles and responsibilities and any agreements or arrangement that may exist on the subject. Union officials seeking time off should give management as much advance notice as is reasonable in the circumstances, indicating "the nature of the business for which time off is required, the intended location and the expected periods of absence. Management and the union should seek to agree arrangements, where necessary, for other employees to cover the work of officials taking time off." Where meetings of members in working hours are necessary, arrangements should be agreed with management as far in advance as practicable and, especially where meetings involve a large proportion of employees in the workplace, they should be held at an agreed time which minimises the disruption of work, *e.g.* towards the end of a shift or the working week or close to a meal break. If a number of employees require time off simultaneously, there should be agreement that employees essential to the undertaking's safety or continued effectiveness should remain at work (*e.g.* where premises have to be kept open for the public or to provide manning for some continuous manufacturing process). If postponements of time off are necessary, the employer should make clear his reasons for postponement, and in agreeing alternative times for the performance of the official's duties, the urgency of the need for time off should be balanced against the seriousness of the employer's problems which may arise from granting time off. Those taking time off should not unnecessarily prolong their absence from work, and any disputes or grievances relating to time off should be referred to agreed procedures, which should be consistent with other such procedures existing between the same parties (para. 12).

Industrial action raises difficult problems, since clearly an employer will be unwilling to grant representatives time off for activities that may disrupt his undertaking. The ACAS Code, paras 31-35, emphasises the importance initially of relying on agreed procedures to avoid industrial action, and of maintaining established time off arrangements when communications and co-operation are in danger of breaking down; hasty alteration of time off arrangements at such junctures may render settlement of differences more difficult. Where the representative himself is not involved in his constituents' industrial action (*e.g.* where they have stopped work unofficially without complying with agreed procedures), then normal time off arrangements should apply. Also granting time off may be appropriate where the work of one workplace is affected by industrial action of another workgroup, so that a representative and his constituents can discuss their own attitudes to the issue.

So, as an official, a safety representative is still entitled to paid time off when seeking to negotiate a settlement of a go-slow in which he and his constituents are involved over the use, say, of a dangerous chemical, since he is representing his constituents' complaints (under Reg. 4 (1) (*c*)) or conducting collective bargaining with management (under the ACAS Code, para. 13 (*a*)). However, EPCA, s. 28 (2) excludes rights to time off for union activities which themselves consist of industrial action. A go-slow constitutes industrial action, so the representative's constituents would not be entitled under the ACAS Code to unpaid time off to attend a meeting during working hours to vote on a return to ordinary work; any such time off would have to be specifically agreed with the employer.

Time off for training

Regulation 4 (2) (*b*) provides that employers shall permit representatives to take such time off with pay during the employee's working hours as shall be *necessary* for undergoing such training in aspects of his statutory functions as may be *reasonable in all the circumstances* having regard to any relevant provisions of a Code of Practice approved by the HSC.

Employers are always anxious that time off for training will benefit their undertakings; unions are concerned that training equips representatives to perform their union responsibilities effectively, irrespective of any benefit to employers. Hence the TUC's concern that they or member unions should be responsible for the content of any training course for safety representatives. The HSC Code recommends that as soon as possible after their appointment safety representatives should be permitted time off with pay to attend *basic* training approved by the TUC or by their (independent) union. While the length of training cannot be rigidly prescribed, basic training should take into account the statutory functions of safety representatives.

> "In particular, basic training should provide an understanding of the role of safety representatives, of safety committees, and of trade union policies and practices in

relation to (*a*) the legal requirements relating to the health and safety of persons at work, particularly the group or class of persons they directly represent; (*b*) the nature and extent of workplace hazards, and the measures necessary to eliminate or minimise them; (*c*) the health and safety policy of employers, and the organisation and arrangements for fulfilling those policies. Additionally, safety representatives will need to acquire new skills in order to carry out their functions, including safety inspections, and in using basic sources of legal and official information and information provided by or through the employer on health and safety matters." (HSC "Time Off" Code, para. 4).

In practice basic training is provided by individual unions or by the TUC and usually lasts for five or ten days. Courses generally cater for safety representatives from a number of different undertakings, jobs and unions, so the emphasis is on procedures and approaches of general application, *e.g.* the identification of relevant hazards and welfare problems, the source and application of relevant standards and—through effective workplace organisation—enforcement and improvement of acceptable standards. Some TUC courses, however, do also cater for specific industries (such as construction, local government, foundries, iron and steel) and courses run by individual unions will also more specifically relate to an individual industry.

The Code is less clear-cut about further training: any such training, it states, should be approved by the TUC or the union appointing the safety representative, and should be available to the representative with special responsibilities or where such training is necessary to meet changes in circumstances or relevant legislation. So the HSC seems to assume that the basic training course is normally sufficient to equip safety representatives to perform their duties. In practice, however, representatives will often require further information and training about the situation at their own workplaces. Not only are employers advantageously placed to give much of this further information and (if necessary) training but it also falls within their general duty under HASAWA, s. 2 (2) (*c*) to provide employees with "information, instruction, training, and supervision." So frequently the employer should be the source of information and training about hazards at a workplace. However, additional courses run by unions, industrial advisory committees or outside bodies will also be vital to assess such information and training critically.

The HSC Code's cautiousness on further training and on what amounts to a reasonable amount of time off may handicap representatives' requests for time off for courses other than for basic training. The Code emphasises that it is for the trade union to nominate a safety representative to receive training "relevant to his function" and that it is the union that is responsible for the content of such training although it should "inform management of the course it has approved and supply a copy of the syllabus, indicating its contents, if the employer asks for it." It recommends that employers should be given some weeks' notice of safety representatives nominated for training course, and that the number of representatives attending courses at the same time should be reasonable in the circumstances, bearing in mind such factors as the availability of courses and employers' operational requirements. There should be prior agreement between unions and management on numbers of representatives undergoing training and the overall arrangements for training, any problems being referred to agreed disputes procedures.

Amounts of time off

The Codes' lack of guidance as to what constitutes a reasonable amount of time off makes the conclusion of prior agreements particularly important. However, in the field of health and safety the tendency is merely to agree that the question will be subsequently negotiated or that the amount of time off will be reasonable. This contrasts with the practice with regard to time off for industrial relations functions where a maximum amount of time off for the performance of union representatives' duties may be negotiated in advance by reference to a maximum number of hours per week (or per month or per year); this avoids possibly time-consuming disputes over the right to time off at the actual instant when the time off is required, which may be untimely given the urgency of many health and safety matters. It also means that within that agreed weekly, monthly, or annual period the representative is free to use the time off as he wishes without needing to justify every minute of it to management. However, it may be difficult to predict what are reasonable requirements for time off and hence there may be an inclination to make conservative provision especially when, with safety representatives, there is little previous experience to go on.

The best solution may be to break down the requirements of time off into categories. The first category could be time off for a representative's routine duties (*e.g.* inspections, report-writing, studying new publications, etc.) for which a reasonably accurate amount of time off can be agreed in advance on a regular weekly, fortnightly or monthly basis. Then an assessment of the amount of time off for ad hoc duties can be calculated by reference to a weekly, etc., period. The final category will have to be dealt with by agreement as and when the need arises, although even then the overall agreement can settle the general principles under which such time off can be requested and granted, *e.g.* the need for supervisors' permission before safety representatives can leave their place of work on trade union business. Many of these principles will be covered by the matters mentioned in the ACAS Code discussed above.

Finally, problems over time off can, of course, always be avoided by the appointment of full-time safety representatives.

Pay during time off

The Schedule to the Regulations lays down minimum rates of pay for representatives during periods of time off. The calculation of pay depends on whether the representative is normally paid at a fixed hourly rate or at a rate which varies with the amount of work done (*e.g.* where the representative is on piecework or his pay includes commission or tips). Representatives paid at fixed hourly rates receive pay during time off as if they had worked at their normal work during that period of time off; representatives paid at variable rates receive their average hourly earnings for that work during periods of time off. Such average hourly earnings are the average hourly earnings of the safety representative concerned; or (if no fair estimate can be made of such earnings) the average hourly earnings received by workers of the same kind as the representative employed in comparable work by the same employer; or (in the absence of such comparable employee) a figure of average hourly earnings which is reasonable in the circumstances.

As already mentioned a safety representative may be permitted time off either under the Regulations or under EPCA, s. 27 (formerly EPA, s. 57). Accordingly the Schedule provides that an employer is not liable to pay representatives twice over, under the Regulations *and* EPCA or under any other contractual obligation in respect of the same period of time off.

Complaints to industrial tribunals of refusal of time off or failure to pay

Refusal to grant a representative time off or to pay him in accordance with the Regulations can give rise to a complaint to an industrial tribunal. This is the sole exception to the Regulations' lack of any direct sanctions for non-compliance. So refusal to grant time off, with its possibility of complaint to an industrial tribunal, may be also used as an indirect means of complaining about other matters, such as an employer's refusal to negotiate with a safety representative nominated by a recognised trade union or a difference of opinion as regards the appropriate number of representatives in a workplace (see Chap. 2). Such indirect means of enforcement may be particularly useful for a recognised union unwilling or unable to exert industrial pressure.

The three month period for filing complaints, the procedure before industrial tribunals, and their remedies are identical to time-off cases under EPCA (for which see the Law at Work title *Union Members*). If the representative proves that the complaint of refusal to grant time off is well founded, the tribunal must make a declaration to that effect. Additionally it may order the employer to compensate the representative.

4 The Functions of Safety Representatives (1)—Communications

The statutory functions

A safety representative has functions specified by HASAWA and the Regulations. HASAWA, s. 2 (4) and (6) provides that he shall represent the employees in connection with the employer's duties to carry out consultations with a view to making and maintaining arrangements which will enable employers and employees to co-operate effectively in promoting and developing employees' health and safety at work, and in checking the effectiveness of such measures. This vague language has to be read alongside the following categories of functions prescribed by the Regulations:

(1) *Rights of representation on behalf of employees*

- (a) Representations to the employer on general matters affecting the health, safety or welfare at work of employees at the workplace (Reg. 4 (1) (*d*));
- (b) Representations to the employer on matters arising from investigations (see (d) below);
- (c) Representations in consultations at the workplace with HSE or local authority inspectors (Reg. 4 (1) (*f*)).

(2) *Rights to receive information*

- (a) from inspectors under HASAWA, s. 28 (8) (Reg. 4 (1) (*g*))
- (b) from employers:
  - (i) information, within the employer's knowledge,

which is necessary to enable safety representatives to fulfil their functions (Reg. 7 (2) subject to exceptions listed there and in Reg. 7 (3)); and

(ii) to inspect and take copies of any document relevant to the workplace or to his constituents which the employer is statutorily required to keep, unless it relates to the health records of an identifiable individual (Reg. 7(1)).

(3) *Rights of inspection*

(a) Routine inspections of the workplace (Reg. 5 (1))

(b) Ad hoc inspections:

(i) after substantial changes in the conditions of work or the publication of new information by the HSC or HSE relevant to hazards of the workplace (Reg. 5 (2))

(ii) after notifiable diseases or accidents or dangerous occurrences at the workplace (Reg. 6).

(4) *Rights of investigation*

(a) of potential hazards and dangerous occurrences and to examine the causes of accidents at the workplace (Reg. 4 (1) (*a*)); and

(b) of complaints by any constituents relating to his own health, safety or welfare at work (Reg. 4 (1) (*b*)).

(5) *Rights in connection with safety committees*

(a) The employer's obligation to establish a safety committee within three months of two safety representatives' written request (HASAWA, s. 2 (7) and Reg. 9 (1); and

(b) The right for safety representatives to be consulted by employers establishing safety committees (Reg. 9 (2) (*b*)).

(c) The right to attend safety committee meetings in his capacity as safety representative in connection with any of his prescribed functions (Reg. 4 (1) (*h*)).

These functions are further expanded or limited by recommendations contained in the Code and Guidance Notes. They may also be expanded (and perhaps limited—see p. 29) by agreement or by other legislation (*e.g.* as regards time off—see p. 34); indeed frequently the prescribed functions merely provide a framework for more extensive rights.

This and the next two chapters discuss the functions of safety representatives in greater detail. This chapter is devoted to "communication functions" which cover rights of representation and rights to receive information (categories (1) and (2) above). Chapter 5 deals with rights of investigation and inspection (categories (3) and (4) above), and Chapter 6 deals with rights connected with safety committees (category (5)).

The communications functions of safety representatives

The most important communications occur between management and safety representatives. Employers may "consult" representatives to seek factual information or constituents' reactions to a management proposal. Representatives may "represent" an individual constituent or their whole constituencies or may make representations affecting even non-constituents in their workplaces (Reg. 4 (1) (*c*) and (*d*)); and representations may include, say, requests for protective clothing, protests about working conditions, or demands for the withdrawal of an allegedly toxic substance. Representatives should "bring to the employer's notice normally in writing any unsafe or unhealthy conditions or working practices or unsatisfactory arrangements for welfare at work," although matters of urgency may, in the first instance, be reported orally (Code, para. 5 (*c*)).

One justification for restricting the appointment of statutory safety representatives to recognised trade unions is that such unions have existing channels of communication with management, their members and officials, and with other unions. In these ways a safety representative is ideally placed for the transmission of health and safety information both within his workplace and in the wider undertaking. Where there are a large number of safety representatives in an undertaking, it may be convenient that one representative receives information from the employer and then passes it on to all the other safety representatives. A similar process can apply for the representation to management of employees' views which are common to different workplaces and/or unions.

The remainder of this chapter examines these points of contact between a safety representative and management, his union, its members, the inspectorate, and other bodies.

The communication of information and the employer

Employers must provide such information as is practicable to ensure the health and safety at work of *all* their employees, and bring the written statement of their health and safety policy to the notice of all employees (HASAWA, 2 (2) (*c*) and (3)). Safety representatives should take all reasonable steps to keep themselves informed of such policy (the Code, para. 5 (*a*) (iii)). A statement of policy should first of all state the undertaking's basic health and safety objectives. Then, either in the statement itself or by reference to other documents, it should spell out in greater detail the organisation and arrangements adopted to put this policy into effect, e.g.

(a) The duties and responsibilites for health and safety of (specified) line managers, with their names and locations, including the director (or equivalent officer) in the undertaking with overall responsibility for health and safety. Those with key responsibilities should be readily available at all material times or have properly nominated and qualified deputies.

(b) The functions of the safety manager and/or safety officers, their relationships to the board of directors (or equivalent body) and to line managers.

(c) The standards to be observed for plant, machinery, chemicals, substances, housekeeping, etc.

(d) Safety procedures to be observed (*e.g.* in the operation of machines, use of dangerous tools or materials, and the wearing of protective masks, etc.).

(e) Arrangements to deal with all identified potential hazards (*e.g.* procedures for storage, transport, packing, labelling, use and disposal of toxic chemicals).

(f) Systems for monitoring safety performance, including inspections, and for publicising the resulting information, including the intervals at which such information is published and to whom it is circulated.

(g) Systems for emergencies such as fires and major accidents, and the arrangements for mock procedures and fire drills to prepare for such incidents.

(h) Arrangements for training new and existing employees and supervisory staff in recognition and avoidance of dangerous hazards, and in emergency procedures.

(i) Any arrangements relating to the appointment and functions of safety representatives and safety committees.

Regulations also require employers to exhibit at the principal entrance (or some other suitable place, where more appropriate) a notice specifying the arrangements he has made to safeguard the health and safety of his employees, and details of the organisation of the relevant inspectorates and the EMAS.

Representatives also need more information than is available to employees generally, so employers must make available to safety representatives the information within their knowledge, necessary to enable them to fulfil their functions (*e.g.* Reg. 7 (2)), and the Code, para. 6, spells out the following implications of the Regulation. Information necessary for representatives includes:

(a) "information about the plans and performance of the employer's undertaking and any changes proposed in so far as they affect the health and safety at work of their employees."

So an employer should disclose to representatives such matters as proposed purchases of new machinery, new processes or layouts of plant, increased production rates, even changes in payment systems, if they will affect employees' health and safety. Clearly these provisions go near to introducing a degree of employee participation in many undertakings' planning procedures (see Chap. 5).

(b) "information of a technical nature about hazards to health and safety and precautions deemed necessary to eliminate or minimise them in respect of machinery, plant, equipment, processes, systems of work and substances in use at work."

Technical information may not be readily comprehensible by non-specialist safety representatives who may therefore require further explanations from the employer or experts within the union or outside. The latter possibility, of course, could lead to the spread of information which the employer would prefer kept confidential. Where use of outside experts is necessary, employers and representatives should do so together and agree as to whom to consult. If representatives wish to have advice from their own technical advisers, they may do so with the employer's prior agreement; the experts' resulting report should be made available to the employer (GN 26).

The employer must also pass on relevant information provided by consultants, manufacturers, importers, or suppliers of any article or substance used or to be used at work by their employees (Code, para. 6 (*b*)). So purchasing departments must pass on manufacturers' and others' explanatory instruction manuals, labels and data sheets accompanying potentially hazardous machinery, articles and substances to those employees who will use them. Failure of an employee in a purchasing department to do this could also mean that he himself is in breach of his duty under HASAWA, s. 7 (see p. 4). However, if a manufacturer supplies a dangerous article to an employer without any instructions or with unintelligible information, it is the manufacturer who will be primarily in breach of his general duty to eventual users (HASAWA, s. 6 (see p. 4)).

(c) "information which the employer keeps relating to the occurrence of any accident, dangerous occurrence or notifiable industrial disease and any statistical records" relating to such matters.

Representatives are also entitled, on giving reasonable notice to their employers, to inspect and take copies of any document relevant to their constituency which the employer is statutorily required to keep *except a document consisting of or relating to any health record of an identifiable individual* (Reg. 7 (1)). (Statutes requiring the keeping of records include the Factories Act 1961, the Offices, Shops and Railway Premises Act 1963, and 29 other statutes listed in HASAWA, Sched. 1.) When taking copies, representatives should bear in mind the time it will take employers to produce documents for copying (GN 25).

In combination, these provisions may place safety representatives in a dilemma. Clearly information relating to accidents, dangerous occurrences and diseases is useful for monitoring an employer's health and safety at work record. However, under the Factories Act 1961, for instance (now being replaced by new regulations in operation since January 1, 1980), employers' registers of notifiable accidents, occurrences and diseases are compiled by reference to identifiable individuals; they therefore comprise information which the employer can withhold unless the individual concerned consents to its disclosure.

The employer's solution is to give representatives the information in statistical form without reference to identified or identifiable individuals. Indeed, when the employer himself compiles records of such incidents as part of his obligation to review periodically his arrangements for health and safety, the presentation will normally be purely statistical, and safety representatives will be among those entitled to copies.

(d) "any other information specifically related to matter, affecting the health and safety at work of his employees, including the results of any measurements taken by the employer or persons acting on his behalf in the course of checking the effectiveness of his health and safety arrangements."

Employers must therefore pass on to representatives the results of any tests, analyses or surveys carried out by or on behalf of, management as part of its checks of health and safety arrangements in the workplace. This entitles representatives to do such things as inspect and take copies of records relating to machinery which is regularly inspected. Information from inspections, samplings and measurements (*e.g.* as to noise or toxicity levels) may produce over a period a significant pattern on which action can be taken. The right to any other information relating to employees' health and safety means that representatives are entitled to information *within employers' knowledge* which touches their constituencies—including details of any relevant legislation or of HSC and HSE publications, factual written information (*e.g.* reports from consultant engineers, insurance surveyors or work study practitioners), and even the gist of important meetings or conversations. The right to such information may indeed result in a safety representative himself attending discussions with, say, the employer's consultants.

(e) "information on articles or substances which an employer issues to home-workers."

This means that a representative is also entitled to information from the employer with regard to materials supplied to his constituents working from home. Its separate mention is necessary because such workers may not be employees but contractors of the employer, and therefore outside the other provisions which are expressed in terms solely of "employees."

Limitations on representatives' rights to information

Representatives' rights to information from employers *within their knowledge* is subject to qualifications in addition to those mentioned on p. 47; in particular *there is no right to information the disclosure of which would be against the interests of national security* (Reg. 7 (2) (*a*)). This is akin to the general restriction limiting representatives' rights to inspect a place, article, or substance on grounds of national security unless the representative satisfies any requirement imposed by the Crown (Reg. 2 (3)). Both these provisions can considerably restrict the scope of representatives' functions in government departments or plants with defence contracts. Disputes as to whether information affects national security cannot, it seems, be dealt with by collective bargaining since disclosure by the employer, even if solely due to union pressure, may result in breaches of the Official Secrets Acts 1911-39 or of a term relating to confidentiality in a contractor's agreement with the Government. A representative's only response to a contractor's assertion that information cannot be disclosed on security grounds is to seek confirmation from the government department concerned.

There are four other grounds on which an employer may be exempted from disclosing information in Reg. 7 (2):

(i) *Information whose disclosure would involve contravening a statutory prohibition*, which could again justify non-disclosure of information within the Official Secrets Acts.

(ii) *Information relating specifically to an individual, unless he has consented to its disclosure*. It can considerably handicap a representative's investigation if he cannot obtain medical records of individual workers who have come into contact with, say, an allegedly toxic chemical in the course of their work, because the worker concerned is not available or is unwilling to give his consent. Even where an individual is available and consents to disclosure, this may be ineffective because the information is contained in medical records compiled by a company doctor, and the doctor may on grounds of medical etiquette (*not* of law) refuse to disclose them to a third party such as a safety representative. Whether such records are also withheld from the employer seems to vary; certainly if employers have access, there seems no ground of etiquette which could entitle a company doctor to refuse access to representatives who have the patients' consent.

(iii) *Information the disclosure of which would, for reasons other than its effect on health, safety or welfare at work, cause substantial injury to the employer's undertaking.* This is the likeliest exemption to be relied on in practice and to be disputed, especially in view of its uncertain meaning. On the one hand it may exempt an employer from disclosure if the information relates *both* to health and safety *and* to other matters which an employer claims would cause his undertaking substantial injury. In that case an employer's reliance on this exemption could prove highly restrictive to representatives. Alternatively the exemption may merely exempt information which does not relate to health and safety. This interpretation, however seems unlikely because such information does not have to be disclosed by the employer anyway since it is not information "necessary to enable a safety representative to fulfil his function" of representing his workmates in matters of health and safety.

This ambiguity may be resolved by the principle particularly applicable to exemption (iv) below but which could also apply here, namely, that what matters is the dominant purpose for which the document in dispute was prepared. Only if this dominant purpose was for something other than health and safety would the employer be entitled to withhold the document from disclosure.

Alternatively, the representative's union could simply rely on collective bargaining sanctions or the enforcement procedure under EPA, ss. 17-21 (see the Law at Work title *Trade Unions*).

This requires that the information sought but withheld must be (a) information without which a trade union representative would be to a material extent impeded in carrying on collective bargaining with the employer, and (b) information which it would be good industrial relations practice for an employer to disclose (and an ACAS Code of Practice offers guidance as to what constitutes such good practice). If attempts at conciliation are ineffective, and the CAC decides in the union's favour, it states a time by which the employer ought to disclose the information. If the employer continues to withhold this information, the CAC may order that the employment contracts of the representative's constituents should include certain terms and conditions to which the information withheld relates.

So the employer is not ordered to disclose information, but at best his employees may have a new term included in their contracts. This may have been the union's object in requesting the information originally; however, this is not necessarily the case: not every request for information relates to possible terms in employees' contracts, especially where a safety representative seeks general information relating to a work-group, *e.g.* hazards likely in new processes. Nor does the statutory procedure prevent an employer withholding information when it is next requested: it merely imposes pressure to disclose information by causing him trouble and adverse publicity if he does not.

Withholding information is also permissible where the information is supplied to the employer by a third party and disclosure would cause substantial injury to that third party's undertaking (Reg. 7 (2) (*d*)). EPA, s. 18 (1) (*c*) also exempts from disclosure information communicated in confidence to the employer or obtained by the employer as a result of the confidence placed in him by a third party. No such exemption exists under the Regulations; however, all the EPA disclosure provisions extend to safety representatives if they are seeking information for collective bargaining (see p. 14).

In any event there are case-law decisions establishing that a person unjustifiably disclosing another's confidential information can be restrained by the owner of such information from making use of it. There has only been one successful case of breach of confidence reported against trade unionists in Great Britain. So perhaps confidential information is dealt with satisfactorily in practice, partly because the persons likely to benefit from unions' indiscretions will often be employers' competitors, which will work to the harm of everyone—including the work-people. Also many undertakings have developed procedures for communicating information to unions in confidence. So the gap in the Regulations is less significant than it may at first seem.

Increasingly rights to information are negotiated in advance, and frequently included in safety agreements. The wording of these clauses needs careful consideration, since specifying the information to which representatives are entitled may in fact limit their statutory rights to information.

Information agreements may cover the types of information to be disclosed or withheld, procedures for the supply of information (*e.g.* the need for a prior written request of a specified duration), the person to whom such a request is to be made, the ways in which confidential information may be communicated, and persons to whom it may (or may not) be passed on. It may be possible to categorise information into that which should be periodically supplied (*e.g.* regularly available accident or health statistics, records of effluents or waste products, or periodically issued information from the HSC) and other information which should be supplied only on demand (*e.g.* details of contracts with health and safety implications, research findings, and ad hoc samplings).

In the absence of information agreements representatives can compile check-lists of information which they need. Frequently union handbooks offer model lists which can be adapted to suit individual circumstances.

(iv) *Information obtained by an employer for the purpose of legal proceedings* will be exempted from disclosure if the anticipation of legal proceedings is the dominant purpose for the document's preparation. If, however, a report is produced by a safety officer after an accident in order to discover its cause, review safety procedures and anticipate possible litigation, then the pending legal proceedings will not have been the dominant purpose underlying the report's preparation, and its contents cannot be withheld from a representative. Indeed the availability of such information may actively assist any injured employee's claims for compensation.

The communication of information and the representative's constituents

A safety representative not merely obtains information from his employer but passes it on to and receives information back from his constituents. Nevertheless neither HASAWA nor the Regulations mention representatives' communications with their constituents.

Much information regarding, say, hazards in the workplace will come not from the representative's own observations but from his constituents, and it will be they who effectively initiate investigations. In a small workplace it is merely necessary that the representative is readily accessible to receive their communications. For constituents on shift work or working in dispersed shops or offices a more formal communications network is necessary. In representing constituents' individual complaints representatives must observe agreed procedures. So employees should first sort out their difficulties themselves with their foreman or supervisor; if this is unsuccessful representatives should try to resolve matters themselves with the employees' immediate superiors. Subsequently procedures often require representatives to take disputes to the next level of management—at the same time the matter may be raised with shop stewards' or safety representatives' committees or with senior shop stewards and also with undertakings' safety officers. The details and complexity of procedures will vary but at higher stages they are likely to involve full-time officials and a local inspector or EMAS officer. Where the matter is less urgent it may go to the appropriate safety committee before probably involving top management.

In matters of urgency a representative should be involved at the outset. Where an employee is asked to handle a new and possibly dangerous chemical, it may be a matter of relying on a status quo clause so that no change of practice takes place until a satisfactory procedure has been negotiated. In a really hazardous situation employees may need to be advised not to work a machine until it is made safe or replaced. In such cases other officials, more senior levels of management, inspectors and the EMAS will be brought in earlier; and if there are industrial relations implications, ACAS should be consulted.

In disputes involving a number of employees, different procedures may apply with possibly eventual recourse to procedures outside the undertaking provided, for example, by an industrial joint negotiating committee. So far as possible health and safety procedures need to be integrated with existing dispute and grievance procedures to reduce the possibility of conflicts between safety representatives with health and safety interests and shop stewards with industrial relations responsibilities. Nevertheless industrial relations constituencies and health and safety constituencies do not always coincide; and faster-moving procedures may be needed for the speedy settlements that health and safety problems sometimes demand.

The communication of information and the representative's union

Representatives must maintain good two-way relations with local officials of their union. Unions can gather together the health and safety experience of their representatives, establish procedures, and then pass on to individual representatives advice and experience collected from other workplaces. In some disputes, representatives may (see p. 53) need to involve local officials, either to comply with accepted procedures or to draw on their wider negotiating experience. Moreover, where the jobs of safety representatives and shop stewards are separate, close relations with the steward(s) covering the workplace are important to avoid conflict, especially in communicating with their employer and constituents. In practice, shop stewards will often have held office for longer and have dealt with a wider variety of industrial relations problems, so clearly tact is called for if newly-appointed representatives are to benefit from stewards' greater experience.

In multi-union workplaces, representatives should work closely with safety representatives (*and* shop stewards) of other recognised unions. In such circumstances all these unions may establish a safety representatives' committee linked—in a large undertaking—to a similar committee for the whole undertaking. Such committees can ensure that individual safety representatives co-ordinate their activities and especially their individual investigations or "campaigns" into particular hazards. Also, if one representative develops certain specialist skills, his particular experience may benefit a wider circle than his own constituents. In many areas there exist local trade union groups (see p. 77) which may also provide sources of further information and experience.

Communications with the inspectorate

Safety representatives also represent their constituents in consultations with inspectors and in receiving information from them (Reg. 4 (1) (*f*) and (*g*)).

Representatives put their constituents' case at workplace meetings with employers and inspectors. Representatives may accompany inspectors on workplace inspections, and have private discussion with them afterwards. By implication employers must notify safety representatives whenever inspectors are in the workplace—in fact, inspectors will normally insist that safety representatives are notified. The inspectorate also encourages representatives to consult them directly for advice and information.

Representatives are the proper recipients of information which inspectors are statutorily bound to communicate to the workforce. Inspectors must pass on two types of information to help keep employees adequately informed (HASAWA, s. 28 (8)), and such information must also be passed on to employers: (a) factual health and safety information obtained by inspectors in the exercise of their statutory powers (see p. 10) relating in any way to premises in which the employees work; (b) information with respect to any action which inspectors have taken or propose to take in exercising their duties on or in connection with those premises. So if inspectors discover hazards in a workplace from samples taken during an inspection, or propose to dismantle dangerous equipment, and in either case consider that the workers affected need to be informed, then the inspector *must* pass on such information to representatives even though this may cause the disclosure of employers' trade secrets, *e.g.* the ingredients of a manufacturing process. However, such disclosure is entirely a matter for the inspector; if he considers the circumstances do not warrant passing on the information, he is under a positive duty *not* to disclose information obtained from the exercise of his powers (HASAWA, s. 28 (7)).

HASAWA, s. 28 (8), is a rare example of the law putting the priorities of safety above the protection of confidences and trade secrets. Obviously in practice an inspector is likely to communicate the information so that damage to employers' interests is as slight as possible; such caution is encouraged by the restrictions on disclosure in HASAWA, s. 28 (2)-(6). For example, information given by an inspector to a representative should not be disclosed other than to the employer or his constituents without the inspector's consent except where the information is passed on in the course of the representative's statutory functions (HASAWA, s. 28 (3) (*b*)). The use by a representative of such information for other purposes could render him liable to prosecution and, on conviction, to a maximum sentence of two years' imprisonment and/or a fine.

Establishing good relations with inspectors will make handling sensitive information easier than a summary of the strictly legal position might suggest. Such a relationship is clearly harder to establish where a representative's workplace is rarely inspected, especially where lack of occupational illness and accidents makes it difficult to justify more frequent inspections. However, personal contacts can be made with inspectors without the representative's workplace having necessarily been inspected, and at least then representatives know that they can (when necessary) rely on inspectors as an additional source of pressure on employers to comply with their obligations.

Communications with other bodies outside experts, etc.

Although the Regulations scarcely mention contacts with industrial advisory committees, outside experts, research institutes, etc., in practice representatives may need to rely on outside experts from other parts of the undertaking or elsewhere (*e.g.* a local university). These experts may test samples, advise on acceptable standards, or suggest advisable precautions, etc., (see p. 47). In doing so, it is important both on grounds of confidentiality and the maintenance of good relations with employers, that sensitive information is not unnecessarily passed on (see p. 50).

5 The Functions of Safety Representatives (2)—Inspections and Investigations

The right of safety representatives to inspect their workplaces and investigate health, safety and welfare matters on behalf of their constituents involves active participation in matters traditionally seen as the exclusive prerogative of management. These functions, therefore, raise controversial aspects of safety representatives' responsibilities.

The Regulations speak of inspections and investigations as distinct and different operations. The essential difference, however, is that investigations are more general and wide-ranging: a representative may *investigate* potential hazards, dangerous occurrences, and the causes of accidents or a constituent's complaints (Reg. 4 (1) (*a*) and (*b*)) any of which may involve inspecting the workplace, perusing documents, and interviewing witnesses, outside experts and inspectors. In particular, the Regulations do not specify the areas which may be inspected, the people who may participate, or the facilities the employer may be required to provide.

By contrast inspections fall into two specific categories: routine periodic inspection permitted at three-monthly intervals or more, frequently by agreement (Reg. 5 (1)); and "ad hoc inspections" after a substantial change in the conditions of work, or where new information has been published by the HSC or HSE, or after notifiable accidents, dangerous occurrences or notifiable diseases (Regs. 5 (2) and 6).

The possible confusion arising from the overlap between investigations and inspections makes it advisable to negotiate safety agreements which can lay down safety representatives' rights more precisely (see below). By setting out in advance parties' rights, agreements avoid the possibility of argument coinciding embarrassingly with a serious accident and allow open discussion of the important implications for a workplace's industrial relations of these extensive new rights. This does not, however, mean that inspections inevitably involve conflicts of interest. In recommending a joint approach to inspections, the HSC stresses that the main purpose of an examination of, for example, a machine involved in an accident is "to determine the causes (of the accident) so that the possibility of action to prevent a recurrence can be considered" (GN 25). The role of a safety representative in inspections and investigations, therefore, should not be to allocate blame but to participate in preventive action.

Preparation for investigations and inspections

Before carrying out investigations or inspections safety representatives must have the necessary background information.

First, they must know where they may go. Clearly they are entitled to go round the workplace where they and their constituents work, but the statutory definition of workplace also covers any place where their members are "likely to work or which they are likely to frequent in the course of their employment or incidentally to it" (Reg. 2 (1)). So this covers, say, an accounts office, store-room, or packing department which constituents visit in connection with their jobs, and places such as canteens, rest-rooms, lavatories, and stairs and corridors leading to them, which workers will frequent in the course of employment or incidentally to it. The definition equally applies to workers with a number of different workplaces (*e.g.* maintenance men or refuse collectors).

However, suppose that in a chemicals factory workers in one workplace are affected by fumes escaping from another area which is a place where the workers are unlikely to work or frequent. Under the specific rights of inspection, their representative is not entitled to examine the source of the fumes. There are two

solutions if the employer stands on the strict letter of the Regulations in such circumstances: (a) the safety representative can seek the assistance of the representative of the place from which the fumes are escaping, and ask him to investigate on his behalf; this points to the importance of good relations and communications between safety representatives in different workplaces and, possibly, different unions (see p. 54).
(b) Alternatively (or additionally), the safety representative can rely on his rights to investigate (in this case) "complaints by an employee he represents relating to that employee's health, safety or welfare at work" (Reg. 4 (1) (*b*)), which is phrased sufficiently widely to permit the representative, if necessary, to carry out investigations outside his own workplace. This illustrates how important it may be to know the precise Regulation under which a representative acts, and hence the merit of sorting out in advance representatives' rights to move around their employers' undertakings reasonably freely *whenever circumstances so require*.

Clearly representatives must make practical preparations, such as collecting together any necessary equipment (see p. 62), and compiling checklists, inventories and layout plans of the workplace in order to ensure that inspections are thorough but not protracted. Information needs to be available on matters such as dates of machines' last overhaul, and recent reports of inspectors, safety officers, insurance surveyors and fire officers. In particular, representatives need to know in advance the relevant safe standards (Threshold Limit Values or "TLVs") applicable to machines, chemicals, etc., and have studied records and statistics of accidents and occupational illness in relation to their own and comparable workplaces. Obviously the need for detailed work in advance of inspections varies with different workplaces, and the purpose of the inspection and its execution raises technical rather than legal issues outside the scope of this book.

Matters to be agreed with management prior to inspection

The value of prior agreements has been stressed; this section merely collects together some further points which may be conveniently covered in such agreements.

Safety representatives must generally give reasonable prior notice of their intention to inspect the workplace, and for routine inspections this should be in writing (Reg. 5). No notice is required by the Regulations where inspections are conducted under the general investigatory powers but it is sensible normally to give advance notice to management wherever possible, since it enables representatives to inspect and investigate more effectively than otherwise; so the length of notice required and the person to whom it should be given should be agreed. However, on occasions the value of an inspection may depend on its unexpectedness.

Agreements can provide whether routine inspections occur at more than three-monthly intervals (*e.g.* where there are high levels of hazards) or, conversely, in low-hazard workplaces less frequently. Agreements can also lay down whether the size, the different activities or the levels of risk require workplaces to be divided into a number of sections, to be inspected at different times or with differing degrees of regularity—*e.g.* where one part of the workplace is subjected to a greater degree of hazards than the remainder or to rapidly changing circumstances.

The Regulations are not consistent as to whether representatives can inspect unaccompanied by management: only the Regulations relating to inspections provide that management cannot be precluded from attending, although they also state that representatives shall be supplied with facilities for independent investigation and private discussion with employers. In practice there must generally be advantages for at least routine inspections to have present departmental managers, the safety officer and sometimes also the company doctor or nurse, the works engineer, and even such specialist outsiders as fire officers and radiation experts. Equally the union may (with the employer's consent) find it helpful to have their own experts in attendance. So the membership of inspection parties can also be dealt with in agreements, including those who may attend on an ad hoc basis. It may also be worth stating the maximum size of the party to ensure that inspection parties do not obstruct those at work.

Another matter for agreement may be the times at which inspections should take place, especially where shift work applies.

Generally it is preferable to inspect during working hours so that methods of work can be observed and workers are present to give explanations and answer questions.

Lastly, agreements can specify the facilities to be made available by the employer to members of the inspection team (Regs. 5 (3) and 6 (2)). These may range from protective clothing, goggles, equipment for measuring (*e.g.* noise, temperature, toxicity, and dust levels), cameras and recording equipment, the appropriate keys for locked doors, cupboards and making machinery safe, etc.

Ad hoc inspections

(a) *Inspections following notifiable accidents or diseases or dangerous occurrences (Reg. 6)*

After any of these incidents where it is safe for an inspection to be carried out *and* his constituents' interests may be involved, a safety representative may inspect the part of the workplace concerned *and* (so far as is necessary for deciding its cause) any other part of the workplace. A "notifiable accident" is an accident to an employee causing death, serious personal injury or injury resulting in his being off work for more than three consecutive days excluding the day of the accident and any Sundays. (A serious personal injury is a fracture of the skull, spine, pelvis, or a major bone in the arm or leg, the amputation of a hand or foot, the loss of an eye or any injury which results in the admission of the person injured as a hospital in-patient.) A dangerous occurrence is a "near miss" which does not necessarily cause a personal injury but has the potential to do so. Notifiable diseases are occupational diseases in origin of which notice must be given to the HSE under various statutes.

However, the importance of these definitions is lessened because even if an accident or dangerous occurrence is not notifiable, a representative can investigate following complaints from a constituent or on his own initiative as part of an investigation into potential hazards and dangerous occurrences in the workplace (Reg. 4 (1) (*a*) and (*b*)).

Representatives may need to examine machinery, plant, equipment or substances in order to discover the cause of accidents, occurrences or illnesses; however, sometimes employers have to take urgent remedial or precautionary steps to prevent further hazards before representatives' inspections; in that case they should notify representatives of the action taken and confirm this in writing. Representatives may interview privately persons involved or witnesses of incidents as well as representatives of management, safety officers, experts both inside and outside the undertaking, inspectors and members of EMAS. However, representatives must not interfere with evidence or the testing of any machinery, equipment or substance which could destroy factual evidence before an inspector has had the opportunity to investigate the incident as thoroughly as necessary (GN s. 23 and 24).

Prompt investigation of accidents will often coincide with a period of dislocation and sensitivity; so a representative must know his precise rights. He may inspect the part of the workplace concerned provided it is safe for him to do so and his constituents' interests might be involved. Also he can inspect the rest of the workplace to discover the cause of accidents. So while there may be arguments on grounds of safety or the involvement of constituents' interests, employers cannot prohibit inspections merely because of their inconvenience, nor make inspections conditional on their consent; however, representatives should notify employers of their intention to inspect where this is reasonably practicable.

Representatives may seek interviews at the same time as others are collecting evidence for the possible preparation of a criminal prosecution of the persons responsible for an accident or of a civil claim for damages by the person injured. So representatives may encounter unwillingness to answer questions which could be interpreted as admissions of guilt or liability; and employers may seek to rely on the exemptions from disclosing information obtained for the purpose of defending legal proceedings or information relating specifically to an individual (Reg. 7 (2) (*c*) and (*e*)); others may be able to rely on an equivalent common law privilege from disclosure as regards confidential information of information collected in anticipation of legal proceedings (see p. 52).

(b) *Inspections following substantial changes in the conditions of work (Reg. 5 (2))*

Representatives have the right, after consultation with the employer, to inspect a part of the workplace where there has been a substantial change in the conditions of work since the last routine (*i.e.* usually quarterly) inspection. Representatives' rights to facilities and to consult constituents and experts, and the employer's right to be present are the same as for routine inspections. What amounts to a "substantial change" can clearly give rise to argument but the Regulations give as examples the introduction of new machinery or the publication of new information by the HSC or HSE relevant to the workplace.

This right to inspect *follows* (not precedes) the change in working conditions. However, a representative may be so totally opposed to his constituents' use of, say, a new chemical that *after* its introduction by management into a manufacturing process, he may feel his only option is to ban its further use which could lead to a complete stoppage of work. This possibility can be avoided if representatives are consulted *before* the introduction of substantial changes (see the Code, para 6 (*a*)).

This Regulation (and the rights to prior information) have wide implications in view of the range of things that may fall within the phrase "substantial change" and especially the now steady stream of publications and guidance produced by the HSC and HSE. This indicates the importance of representatives keeping up-to-date with these official publications as part of their task to take all reasonably practicable steps to keep informed of the legal requirements relating to their constituents' health and safety, the hazards of their workplaces, and measures necessary to eliminate or minimise risks deriving from these hazards (Code, para. 5 (*a*)).

There may also be wider industrial relations implications since substantial changes in the conditions of work can involve re-deployment of workers or redundancies in addition to matters affecting safety. For instance, the introduction of a new machine or process, such as the installation of visual display units (VDUs) in offices, may reduce employers' needs for clerical staff which union representatives will want to resist, quite apart from their concern for possible effects on their constituents' eyes and general health. The rights to consultation on safety aspects of the introduction of such equipment under the Regulations may in effect give union representatives rights of consultation or, perhaps, rights to negotiate, say, the consequent re-deployment of workers which may be outside the previous scope of that union's recognised bargaining rights.

The conduct of inspections

The conduct of inspections depends on the circumstances of the particular workplace and the kind of inspection involved. Whatever kind of inspection is involved, general alertness will, in the first instance usually be the best means of detecting faults or potential hazards such as frayed power cables, fumes, or unusual colour of dust. These features may often be more noticeable to a stranger than to someone who frequents the workplace every day. Workers will be useful sources of information, especially younger or newer workers whose opinions and expections have not been dulled by over-familiarity or apathy. On a routine inspection the aim is to gain a better understanding of the *overall* maintenance of health and safety at the workplace; they may take a number of forms, and it is for representatives to agree which is appropriate with the employer. The HSC, however, consider that one or more of a combination of the following types of inspection, or all of them, over a period of time may be appropriate: (a) safety tours, *i.e.* general inspections of the workplace; (b) safety sampling, *i.e.* systematic sampling of particular dangerous activities, processes or areas; (c) safety surveys, *i.e.* general inspections of particular dangerous activities, processes or areas (GN 19). Lastly, both representatives and employers should be prepared to take notes, and, if agreed between them, this can subsequently avoid much unnecessary argument. The novelty in many undertakings of workplace inspections by workers' representatives means that ineptitude in such matters may cause needless damage to industrial relations.

Reports and follow-up action

Inspections are likely to lead to further action: joint inspections obviously call for prompt discussion, while completion of routine or ad hoc inspections should be formally recorded by representatives, and will frequently require employers to take follow-up action. Following routine inspections, the form which discussions should take and the responsibility for action should be agreed in advance.

Writing reports, notification of hazards to the employer, discussions (or negotiations) with regard to remedial action, and the carrying out of remedial action are the main forms of action that may need to be taken: all depends on the type of inspection or investigation involved, and its outcome. Clearly many joint inspections lead straight on to discussions between representatives of management and unions, and may involve both immediate remedial action and longer term analysis of working methods. In a multi-union workplace any follow-up action may call for prior discussion by a safety representatives' committee.

Representatives should bring to employers' attention, usually in writing, any unsafe or unhealthy conditions or working practices discovered by an inspection. However, such reports do not imply that all other conditions, working practices, and welfare arrangements are satisfactory. Nor does the requirement of a written report preclude bringing matters to an employer's attention orally in the first instance, particularly where speedy remedial action is necessary or where only a minor matter is in issue (Code, para. 5 (*c*)). Representatives' reports may also be considered by safety committees (Safety Committee Guidance Note ("SCGN") 17. See Chap. 6), and often representatives need to report their findings to their unions and other safety representatives.

The HSC suggests forms for recording that inspections have taken place and for notifying the employer of unsatisfactory findings; and both are obtainable from HSE offices (GN 14). However, their use need not be confined to specific inspections; also forms more suited to inspections and investigations at individual workplaces may be adopted. If non-standard forms are used, it is obviously convenient to agree their contents and lay-out in advance. One possibility is to use an inspection checklist (see page 60) as form of report with additional spaces inserted for follow-up action requested by safety representatives and for the remedial action taken in response (or for explanations by management if such action is not taken).

For reports to lead to effective and prompt action, it must be clear to whom they should be submitted. This person must have sufficient authority to ensure that the requisite remedial action is taken and, if relevant, within a stated time period. His name should be listed in the employer's safety policy (see p. 45).

Representatives are entitled to written explanations of an employer's failure either to take appropriate or acceptable remedial action or to take it within a reasonable time (GN 21); provision is made for this on the HSE form. Once again different forms may be preferred. Where remedial action has been taken, the safety representative should re-inspect to see that matters are now satisfactory; and again he should be able to record his views. The remedial action should be publicised throughout the workplace and any other appropriate parts of the undertaking (GN 22), and safety committees should also be informed.

Following inspections and investigations there may be disagreements about the existence or seriousness of defects or the appropriate remedial measures. Obviously where safety representatives take a more serious view of deficiencies than employers it is likely that representatives will also be dissatisfied with employers' remedial action.

During the first few months of a safety representative's appointment inspections, investigations and their follow-up will be occasions when employers and representatives test out their relationships and the procedures they are going to rely upon. The weight that a safety representative will carry in the long term in relation to his employer, his constituents, and his fellow officials will largely depend on the way he handles his duties in these first months. So representatives must neither exaggerate nor minimise their powers especially on the first few occasions when issues of importance arise.

6 The Functions of Safety Representatives (3)—Their Attendance at Safety Committees

HASAWA and the Regulations cover both safety representatives and safety committees, but this book is only concerned with safety committees to the extent that safety representatives are involved in their work. Safety committees have in many undertakings existed for a considerable time with very varied status and tasks; and neither the Robens Report nor HASAWA, with their emphasis on involving the workforce in health and safety by means of safety representatives, have necessarily altered committees' pre-1974 position.

Where such "voluntary" safety committees continue, their relationship with safety representatives is regulated by the arrangements developed in that particular undertaking. So it is difficult to generalise about the relationship of safety representatives with safety committees except to emphasise that the extent of a representative's rights (as discussed in the previous chapters of this book) should not be affected unless he or his union have agreed by practice or negotiation to the variation of such rights.

However, where no safety committee exists or where it is unsatisfactory, safety representatives may request their employer to establish a "statutory" safety committee under HASAWA, s. 2 (7) and Regulation 9, as amplified by a separate set of Guidance Notes. In such instances, there is more scope for discussing the inter-relationship of committee and representative.

The establishment of statutory safety committees

Two representatives, not necessarily from the same workplace or union, may request their employer in writing to form a safety committee (HASAWA, s. 2 (7) and Reg. 9) based normally on a single establishment (SCGN 5); and the employer *must* set up such a committee within three months of the request. However, in other respects the initiative remains with employers. The employer must "consult" the initiating representatives and other representatives of recognised independent trade unions with members in workplaces to be covered by the proposed committee but the subject-matter of such consultation is left unspecified (Reg. 9). So although it is recommended that detailed arrangements necessary to establish a statutory safety committee should evolve from discussion and *negotiation* between employers and safety representatives (SCGN 3), employers may still insist on setting up committees unilaterally.

It is also recommended that the work of safety committees should be kept separate from works committees—and presumably any other joint negotiating bodies—and that safety matters should not be included on the agenda of other meetings (SCGN 4). By contrast many unionists would object if safety committees were not integrated into existing bargaining structures. In fact, the HSC's advice seeks merely to ensure that health and safety remains an important issue in its own right; it does not say that health and safety may not become subjects of bargaining. It leaves that question entirely to the parties.

So when requesting the establishment of safety committees, representatives should work out in advance what they want the committee to do, how it should conduct its business, and how it should fit into existing bargaining *and* health and safety arrangements. Their proposals should be previously agreed with their constituents so that an employer reluctant to adopt proposals will be aware that they have widespread support. In this way arrangements on such basic matters as the committee's constitution, membership, functions and methods of work are likely to be the outcome of acceptable compromises.

The SC Guidance Notes have some helpful advice on all these matters, which should be studied by representatives contemplating the establishment of a statutory committee or the reorganisation of a voluntary committee. Limitations of space prevent their discussion here, and in any case, they stress that any arrangements made must suit their individual undertakings, (SCGN 2 and 3). Hence the remaining sections of this chapter concentrate solely on points that are likely to impinge on the work of safety representatives as described in the previous two chapters.

Safety committees' functions

Despite their name, safety committees should be concerned with all aspects of health, safety and welfare in the working environment. HASAWA, s. 2 (7) emphasises committees' monitoring role: they should keep under review the measures taken to ensure employees' health and safety, and one of a committee's *agreed* objectives should be the promotion of co-operation between employers and employees in instigating, developing and carrying out measures to ensure employees' health and safety (SCGN 6).

Certain specific monitoring and policy-making functions are suggested including the study of statistics and trends relating to accidents and notifiable diseases; the examination of safety audit reports, information and reports from the inspectorates and safety representatives; assistance in developing works' safety rules, safe systems of work, safety training, and communications and publicity on safety and health; and links with the inspectorates (SCGN 7). Safety committees may in certain instances themselves carry out inspections but it is management's responsibility to take executive action and to check health and safety precautions regularly and effectively (SCGN 8); and safety committees should supplement these functions, not replace them. So by implication it is safety representatives who should perform the watchdog function of ensuring employers' more detailed compliance with their obligations.

Membership of safety committees

A statutory function of safety representatives is to *attend* meetings of safety committees in connection with their other statutory functions (Reg. 4 (1) (*h*)). This does not mean that safety representatives must be members of the committee; nor indeed need such attendance be limited to statutory safety committees, although in practice a representative may not be able to gain access to a voluntary committee in the face of an employer's objection. Membership of statutory committees should be a matter for *consultation* between management and union representatives "through the use of the normal machinery" (SCGN 9); compact committees are recommended which adequately represent both the interests of management and *all* employees, *including* safety representatives. So it seems that some (if not all) safety representatives can attend meetings, although they will not all necessarily have a vote.

The representation of additional employees on safety committees may give non-unionised employees or members of non-recognised unions their best chance of making their views known. If, however, the committee engages in bargaining, conceding such employees' representative capacities could amount to their recognition to the minimum extent required in order to be entitled to appoint safety representatives (see p. 15). So an employer may need to handle a committee's membership and agenda with care.

Membership of safety committees should be regarded as part of an individual's normal work so that employees should suffer no loss of pay through attending meetings or other activities of the committees. However, the Regulations themselves make no separate provision for paid time off; so safety representatives' claims for paid time off must be for time off for performing his statutory functions (see p. 33), which include "*attendance*" at meetings of safety committees. Nevertheless, it seems unlikely that a safety representative deputed, say, to carry out an *investigation* on the committee's behalf, would then be denied paid time off by his employer, or that, if such should be the case, an industrial tribunal would be sympathetically inclined to the employer's case (see p. 41). It also seems unlikely that an employer would refuse a non-unionist member of the committee paid time off; were he to do so, however, the employee would have no right of complaint to an industrial tribunal, since even under the wider provisions of EPCA, ss. 27 and 28, rights to time off are confined to members of independent recognised trade unions.

The inter-relationship of safety committees and safety representatives

Safety representatives and safety committees are appointed independently of each other. Nevertheless their relationship should be "flexible but intimate"; neither is responsible to the other, but they should form the most effective organisation appropriate to individual undertakings and, particularly, create a system of effective co-ordination between their respective areas of work (SCGN 12).

For safety representatives working out their relationship to safety committees, the practical implications of this vague advice is unclear. Certainly a committee's study of workplace trends and accident statistics will be of considerable value to a representative. Indeed, a committee which actively produces this kind of information can usefully do much of a representative's fact-finding work for him, leaving him perhaps to campaign for consequent changes suggested by the statistics.

Safety committees are the places within an establishment where those with major responsibilities and interests in health and safety are likely to meet; they also provide a place where proposals for change can be put. So where a number of representatives are present, they can lend each other weight when a request is made by one of their number, for example, by citing evidence of similar needs in their constituencies. If these advantages are to be effectively realised in an establishment of any size, there must also be a degree of consultation among safety representatives before any meeting of the safety committee.

A safety committee may therefore provide a useful forum for sharing experience and information, for example, with regard to reports and information from such experts as HSE inspectors and safety officers. Discussions by committees of such matters as reviews of works rules, safety procedures, or internal training can provide representatives with additional opportunities for influencing policy-making. So committees enlarge safety representatives' opportunities for gathering information and communicating constituents' views. In this respect alone the opportunities for contact with representatives of management, and others, such as outside experts, may justify the establishment of a committee; there is also the advantage for a safety representative of seeing his particular responsibilities for health and safety from a different and perhaps broader viewpoint.

Safety committees, integrated into the arrangements of which safety representatives themselves form part, can be a useful means of extending safety representatives' effectiveness. The reverse applies if the functions of safety representatives and committees conflict. In that case, it may be noted that the Regulations, Code and SC Guidance Notes make no provision for safety representatives to request the committee's dissolution or reconstitution. Once again, such difficulties must be resolved by collective bargaining if a safety committee is to retain credibility with workers.

Further Information

USEFUL ADDRESSES

HSC/HSE headquarters: Baynard's House, 1 Chepstow Place, London W2 4TF. Tel: 01-229 3456

EMAS headquarters: 25 Chapel Street, London NW1 5DT. Tel: 01-262 3277

In the first instance, inquiries should be made to HSE Area Offices or to Senior Employment Medical Advisers. The area offices of the EMAS share buildings with HSE Area Offices:

HSE Area, Address and Telephone No. (* indicates also office of EMAS)	*Area Covered*	*EMAS Area*
London NW. Chancel House, Neasden Lane, London NW10 2UD. Tel: 01-459 8844.	Barnet, Brent, Camden, City of London, Enfield, Hammersmith, Harrow, Hillingdon, Kensington and Chelsea, Westminster	London and South East
London NE. Maritime House, 1 Linton Road, Barking, Essex IG11 8HE. Tel: 01-594 5522.	Barking, Hackney, Haringey, Havering, Islington, Newham, Redbridge, Tower Hamlets, Waltham Forest	
London S. *1 Long Lane, London SE1 4PG. Tel: 01-407 8911.	Bexley, Bromley, Croydon, Greenwich, Kingston, Lambeth, Lewisham, Merton, Richmond, Southwark, Sutton, Wandsworth	
South East. 3 East Grinstead House, London Road, East Grinstead, West Sussex RH19 1RR. Tel: 0342 26922.	Kent, Surrey, East Sussex, West Sussex	

HSE Area, Address and Telephone No. (*indicates also office of EMAS)	*Area Covered*	*EMAS Area*
South. Priestley House, Priestley Road, Basingstoke RG24 9PW. Tel: 0256 3181.	Berkshire, Dorset, Hampshire, Isle of Wight, Wiltshire	South West
South West. *Intercity House, Mitchell Lane, Bristol BS1 6AN. Tel: 0272 290681.	Avon, Cornwall, Devon, Gloucestershire, Somerset, Isles of Scilly	
West Midlands. *McLaren Building, 2 Masshouse Circus, Queensway, Birmingham B4 7NP. Tel: 021-236 5080.	West Midlands	West Midlands
Marches. 2 Hassell Street Newcastle-under-Lyme, Staffs ST5 1DT. Tel: 0782 625324.	Hereford and Worcester, Salop, Staffordshire	
Wales. *Brunel House, 2 Fitzalan Road, Cardiff CF2 1SH. Tel: 0222 497777.	Clywd, Dyfed, Gwent, Gwynedd, Mid Glamorgan, Powys, South Glamorgan, West Glamorgan	Wales
East Anglia. 39, Baddow Road, Chelmsford, Essex CM2 0HL. Tel: 0245 84661.	Essex except the London Boroughs in Essex covered by London NE, Norfolk, Suffolk	Eastern and South Eastern Midlands
Northern Home Counties. 14 Cardiff Road, Luton. Tel: 0582 34121.	Bedfordshire, Buckinghamshire, Cambridgeshire, Hertfordshire	
East Midlands. Belgrave House, 1 Greyfriars, Northampton NN1 2LQ. Tel: 0604 21233.	Leicestershire, Northamptonshire, Oxfordshire, Warwickshire	

HSE Area, Address and Telephone No. (*indicates also office of EMAS)	*Area Covered*	*EMAS Area*
North Midlands. Birkbeck House, Trinity Square, Nottingham NG1 4AU. Tel: 0602 40712.	Derbyshire, Lincolnshire, Nottinghamshire	North East
South Yorkshire. Sovereign House, 40, Silver Street, Sheffield S1 2ES. Tel: 0742 739081.	Humberside, South Yorkshire	North East
West and North Yorkshire. *8 St. Paul's Street, Leeds LS1 2LE. Tel: 0532 446191.	North Yorkshire, West Yorkshire	North East
Greater Manchester. *Quay House, Quay Street, Manchester M3 3JB. Tel: 061-831 7111.	Greater Manchester	North West
Merseyside. The Triad, Stanley Road, Bootle, L20 3PG. Tel: 051-922 7211.	Cheshire, Merseyside	North West
North West. Victoria House, Ormskirk Road, Preston PR1 1HH. Tel: 0772 59321.	Cumbria, Lancashire	North West
North East. *Government Buildings, Kenton Bar, Newcastle-upon-Tyne. Tel: NE1 2YX. Tel: 0632 869811.	Cleveland, Durham, Northumberland, Tyne and Wear	Northern
Scotland East. *Meadowbank House, 153 London Road, Edinburgh EH8 7AU. Tel: 031-661 6171.	Borders, Central Fife, Grampian, Highland, Lothian, Tayside, and Orkney and Shetland	Scotland
Scotland West. 314 St. Vincent Street, Glasgow G3 8XG. Tel: 041-204 2646.	Dumfries and Galloway, Strathclyde, the Western Isles	Scotland

Organisations

British Safety Council, 62 Chancellor's Road, London W6. Tel: 01-841 1231/2371.

British Society for Social Responsibility in Science, 9 Poland Street, London W1V 1BQ. Tel: 01-437 2728.

British Standards Institution, 2 Park Street, London W1A 2BS. Tel: 01-629 9000 (Postal sales: 101 Pentonville Road, London N1. Tel: 01-837 880).

The Industrial Society, PO Box 1BQ, Robert Hyde House, 48 Bryanston Square, London W1H 1BQ. Tel: 01-262 2401.

International Labour Office, 87/91 New Bond Street, London W1Y 9LA. Tel: 01-499 2084.

The Royal Society for the Prevention of Accidents, Cannon House, The Priory, Queensway, Birmingham B4 6BS. Tel: 021-233 2461.

TUC Centenary Institute of Occupational Health, London School of Hygiene and Tropical Medicine, Keppel Street, London WC1 7HT. Tel: 01-580 2386.

TUC Medical Adviser, TUC, Congress House, Great Russell Street, London WC1B 3LS. Tel: 01-636 4030.

Workers' Educational Association, 9 Upper Berkeley Street, London W1H 8BY.

Local trade union health and safety groups

A number of such groups have been established throughout the United Kingdom to enable safety representatives to share their experiences and to provide information and advisory services (*e.g.* libraries, and lectures by local health and safety experts). For further information about new and established groups, see *Hazards Bulletin* and the *Health and Safety Information Bulletin* (see Periodicals below).

Bedford Association for Safety and Health (BASH), 146 Spring Road, Kempston, Bedford. Tel: 0234 66755.

Birmingham Regional Union Safety and Health Campaign (BRUSH), 160 Corisande Road, Selly Oak, Birmingham 29.

Cannock Health & Safety Experiment (CHASE), 56 Grange Crescent, Penkridge, Staffs.

Coventry Health & Safety Movement (CHASM), Charterhouse, London Road, Coventry.

Doncaster (HASSARD), 29 High Street, Arksy, Doncaster DN5 0SI.

Dunfermline (DASH), Clackmannon House, Clackmannon.

Leeds Action on Safety and Health (LASH), 29 Blenheim Terrace, Leeds 2. Tel: 39633.

North London Health and Safety Group, c/o Camden Community Law Centre, 146 Kentish Town Road, London NW1 9QG. Tel: 01-485 6672.

South London Action on Safety and Health (SLASH), c/o 506 Brixton Road, London SW9 9EN. Tel: 01-733 4245 ext. 2080 (daytime).

Health and Safety in South East London (HASSEL), 6 Sedgebrook Road, Kidbrooke, London SE3 8LP.

Middlesex Action on Safety and Health (MASH), c/o Hillingdon Community Law Centre, 63 Station Road, Hayes, Middlesex. Tel: 01-573 4021.

East London Health and Safety Group, 32 Roman Close, Rainham, Essex.Tel: 01-592 3000.

Merseyside Hazards Group (MHG), 70 Granville Road, Liverpool 15. Tel: 051-733 6925.

Middlesex Centre for Health and Safety Meetings and Information (Secretary: Bob Fosskett), Middlesex Polytechnic, Capel House, Bullsmoor Lane, Waltham Cross, Herts. EN7 5HR. Tel: 9 719555.

Rotherham WEA H & S Information Service, Chantry Buildings, Corporation Street, Rotherham. Tel: 0709 72121.

Sheffield Trade Union Safety Committee, 312 Albert Road, Sheffield 8. Tel: 0742 584559.

Southampton Work Hazards Advisory Committee, 27 Pointout Road, Bassett, Southampton or 4 Charlton Crescent, Southampton. Tel: 0703 29810.

Telford Health and Safety Group, 67 High Street, Dawley, Telford. Tel: 0952 501484.

List of experts

A list, periodically updated, of experts willing to help with scientific and technical problems is available from the Association of University Teachers, United House, 1 Pembridge Road, London W11 3HJ.

OFFICIAL PUBLICATIONS

HSE area offices distribute free leaflets and keep small stocks of publications. Purchases in quantity should be made through government (HMSO) bookshops (in London, Edinburgh, Cardiff, Manchester, Bristol, Birmingham, and Belfast), or by post to PO Box 569, London SE1 9NH.

The following publications especially concern the subject-matter of this book:

The Factories Act 1961
The Offices, Shops and Railway Premises Act 1963
The Health and Safety at Work Act 1974
The Employment Protection Act 1975
The Employment Protection (Consolidation) Act 1978
The Employment Act 1980

<table>
<tr><td>Safety Representatives and Safety Committees Regulations 1977 No. 500
The Code of Practice on Safety Representatives 1977
Guidance Notes on Safety Representatives 1977
Guidance Notes on Safety Committees 1977</td><td>These are available in one booklet</td></tr>
</table>

Safety Committees—guidance to employers whose employees are not members of recognised unions (HSC 8)
Code of Practice on Time Off for Training of Safety Representatives (HSC 9)
Health and Safety (Enforcing Authority) Regulations (S.I. 1977 No. 746)
Guidance Notes on Enforcement
Guidance Notes on Employers' Policy Statements for Health and Safety at Work.

The following ACAS publications are also available from HMSO:

Codes of Practice on: Disciplinary Practice and Procedures,
Time Off for Trade Union Duties and Activities
Disclosure of Information to Trade Unions for Collective Bargaining Purposes

The *HSC Newsletter* is a useful summary of information and is available on subscription. It is published six times a year. It includes information about new legislation, publications and conferences, accident inquiries, work of industrial advisory groups and working parties, and it reproduces HSC guidance notes and summaries of reports. *Annual Reports* are published by the HSC, HSE, EMAS and by individual inspectorates.

OTHER PUBLICATIONS

In view of this book's non-specialist nature, the list below excludes publications produced by unions, employers' associations and professional organisations which are only available to members or which concentrate on specific hazards or industries. However, many of these more specialist publications also include useful lists of further information.

Books and booklets

Redgrave's Health and Safety in Factories (Butterworths, 23rd ed., 1976).
Redgrave's Offices and Shops (Butterworths, 2nd ed., 1973). (This also covers safety aspects of agriculture, railways, and off-shore installations.)
Encyclopedia of Health and Safety at Work (Sweet & Maxwell) (a looseleaf encyclopedia with an updating service).
Encyclopaedia of Occupational Health and Safety, 2 vols. (International Labour Organisation, 1971).
Monkman, *Employer's Liability* (Butterworths, 9th ed. 1979).

Mitchell, *The Employer's Guide to the Law of Health, Safety and Welfare at Work* (Business Books).
Arscott and Armstrong, *An Employer's Guide to Health and Safety Management* (Kogan Page).
Broadhurst, *The Health and Safety at Work Act in Practice* (Heydon).
Howells and Barrett, *Guide for Managers to the Health and Safety at Work Act* (Institute of Personnel Management).
Heinrich, *Industrial Accident Prevention* (McGraw Hill, 4th ed., 1959).
Handley (ed.), *Industrial Safety Handbook* (McGraw Hill, 1977).
Hunter, *The Diseases of Occupations* (English Universities Press, 5th ed., 1975).
Stellman and Daum, *Work is Dangerous to Your Health* (New York Vintage Books, 1973).
Kinnersley, *The Hazards of Work* (Pluto Press, 1973).
Egan, *Appointment and Functions of Safety Representatives* (New Commercial Publishing Co., 1978);
Egan, *Safety Inspections* (New Commercial Publishing Co., 1978);
Egan, *Safety Policies* (New Commercial Publishing Co., 1979).
TUC, *Handbook on Safety and Health at Work* (2nd ed., 1978).
I.L.O., *Publications on Occupational Health and Safety* (1978).
EEF, *Safety Representatives and Safety Committees.*
Bennett, *Safety Representatives' Guide to Fire Precautions* (Workers' Educational Association).
Cunningham, *Safety Representatives: Shop Floor Organisation for Health and Safety* (Workers' Educational Association).
Labour Research Department, *Guide for Safety Representatives* (1979).
Wrigglesworth, *Guide to the Health and Safety at Work Act* (The Industrial Society).
Portman, *A Pocket Guide for Safety Representatives* (The Industrial Society).
ROSPA, *Safety Representatives.*
British Safety Council, *Safety Representatives: a pocket guide.*
British Safety Council, *Safety Representatives' Checklist.*

Periodicals
(for addresses of publishers where not given, see under Organisations above).

Fire Prevention, the Fire Protection Association, Aldermary House, Queen Street, London EC4N 1TJ.

Health and Safety Information Bulletin, Industrial Relations Services, 67 Maygrove Road, London NW6 2EJ.

Industrial Safety, United Trade Press Ltd, 42-43 Gerrard Street, London W1V 7LP.

The Safety Representative (formerly *Look Out*), ROSPA.

Occupational Health (associated with the Society of Occupational Health Nursing), Bailliere Tindall, 35 Red Lion Square, London WC1R 4SG.

Occupational Safety and Health, ROSPA.

Protection (official journal of the Institution of Industrial Safety Officers), Alan Osborne and Associates, 13 Great James Street, London WC1.

Safety (formerly *Safety and Rescue*), British Safety Council.

Bargaining Report, Labour Research Department, 78 Blackfriars Road, London SE1.

Health and Safety at Work, Maclaren Publishers Ltd, PO Box 109, Davis House, 69-77 High Street, Croydon CR9 1QH.

Hazards Bulletin, British Society for Social Responsibility in Science.

FILMS

Working for Safety: seven 25-minute 16 mm films first shown on BBC TV in autumn 1978 to help safety representatives and others recognise and control hazards and prevent accidents. Available for purchase from Ron Crafts, BBC Enterprises, Villiers House, The Broadway, London W5 2PA Tel: 743-8000 ext. 394 or for hire from BBC Enterprises Film Hire, Woodston House, Oundle Road, Peterborough PE2 9P2. Tel: 0733 52257/8.

Something to do with Safety Representatives: a 20-minute 16 mm film made by ICI available for purchase or hire from Millbank Films Ltd., Thames House North, Millbank, London SW1 4QG Tel: 01-834 4444.

Lists of films on health and safety and of film libraries

Arscott and Armstrong, *An Employer's Guide to Health and Safety Management* (see Publications above) Appendix C.

ROSPA Occupational Safety Film Index.

HSE Film Catalogue.

TRAINING COURSES

In addition to courses organised by the TUC, employers' associations, unions, individual employers and industries, special courses for managers and safety representatives are organised by:

The Industrial Society,

ROSPA,

JIRS, 346 Harrow Road, London W9.

ACKNOWLEDGMENTS

I should like to thank Christopher Pitt, Alan Neal, Bridget Paton and Paul O'Higgins for their advice and constructive criticisms.

I should also like to thank the staff of the following organisations for their assistance and for letting me see copies of their publications relating to safety representatives:

ACTT
ASTMS
Amalgamated Textile Workers Union
AUEW
BIFU
British Safety Council
CBI
EEF
EETPU
EMAS
HSE
ILO
The Industrial Society
IPM
Iron and Steel Trades Confederation
NGA
NALGO
NUM
NUR
National Union of Seamen
ROSPA
SOGAT
TGWU
TUC
USDAW

Index